HONORÉ DAUMIER
selected works

HONORÉ DAUMIER
selected works

edited by BRUCE and SEENA HARRIS

with an appreciation by
FRANK and DOROTHY GETLEIN

BOUNTY BOOKS A Division of Crown Publishers, Inc. New York

Table of Contents

Editors' Introduction

By Bruce and Seena Harris

Comic artists, like comic authors, are usually considered inferior to those who deal with "serious" subjects. What then of Daumier, who was not only a caricaturist but had his artistic merits praised by most of the great critics of the world? Though many people are lacking in specific knowledge about that turbulent period of French history covering the monarchy of Louis-Philippe, the Second Republic, and the Second Empire, many more enjoy and are familiar with Daumier's representations of the pear-shaped Louis-Philippe, the bumbling bourgeois, and the sinister Ratapoil.

Honoré Daumier was born in Marseille in 1808. His father, an artisan, was greatly influenced by Rousseau, and went to Paris to seek his fortune and poetic fame. The family of this dreamer never had enough money to live, and young Daumier was apprenticed at a very early age to a notary. He did not work well at this position, and was sent to work in a bookstore. However, a friend of the family, Alaxandre Lenoir, was impressed with the boy's artistic talent and encouraged him.

The first substantiated works of Daumier appeared in the *Silhouette* of July, 1830. These works celebrate the July Revolution and the fall of Charles X. Soon, however, Daumier became disillusioned with the subsequent government of Louis-Philippe. In December, 1831, he portrayed the citizen-king in the form of a Gargantua, stuffed with the coins of the working class, who, after digesting the money, disgorges it to his favorites. He remained a polemicist for the opposition for the rest of his life, attacking one regime after another.

In 1831, Charles Philipon, a popular caricaturist, with his brother founded *La Caricature*. Daumier soon became Philipon's partner, and the main attraction, turning out lithograph after lithograph—all of them hostile to the new regime. In 1832, Daumier was sentenced to six months in jail for the Gargan-

tua caricature. Because of stringent and repressive press regulations *La Caricature* died, only to be almost immediately reborn as *Le Charivari*. The new journal seemed to be more concerned with everyday life in Paris, rather than with the political situation. But every time the government relaxed its vigilance, Daumier's rapier would slash out again.

For the next forty years Daumier created a minimum of two prints a week. His lithographs number over four thousand. Perhaps he worked so diligently because he had dependents of his own to support. In 1846, he married Marie-Alexandrine Dassy, and his mother lived with them for many years. Daumier, like his father before him, never learned to save and was often deep in debt. Since prints were relatively easy to do and the money came quickly, Daumier found himself creating caricatures and lithographs even though he had decided originally to do other work.

Around 1842, Daumier had decided that painting was his true medium. Yet no one could be found to buy his canvases. Unable to find buyers, he gave them away to other artists. About 1860, it became obvious to the critics and the public alike that the quality of Daumier's lithographs was diminishing. Soon, *Le Charivari,* always his court of last resort, refused to accept more lithographs.

Finally, after three years and much pressure from Daumier's friends, the magazine relented and again began to accept the artist's work. The three-year pause had been good for Daumier, and his work recaptured its verve and élan. But now another specter appeared on the horizon—Daumier's sight began to fail. He had to stop all work in 1872, and his lack of savings once more haunted him. Corot, always a staunch admirer of the artist, bought Daumier's house and presented it to him so that he no longer would have to worry about paying rent. Corot explained this altruistic act by saying, "I did it to make the landlord mad." His nobility was answered by Daumier's touching gratitude when he wrote, "You are the only man from whom I could accept such a gift without blushing."

Daumier died at Valmondois in 1879.

What satiric masterpieces could Daumier have produced if there had been no repressive press laws? Although his paintings are recognized as full of genius and truly before their time, what might he have accomplished if he did not have to earn a living penciling drawings he no longer cared about? His situation is reminiscent of Mark Twain and his gilded age. But perhaps it is foolish to speculate on what might have been, when Daumier has left us such a full legacy of lithographs, drawings, paintings, and sculpture.

This book is an attempt to show the most artistically rich and politically relevant lithographs, and to give the reader a variety of the lesser known drawings, sculpture, and paintings. The essay by Frank and Dorothy Getlein, taken from their excellent book, *The Bite of the Print,* puts Daumier's work in a setting of social significance. We have put the litho-graphs concerned with lawyers and doctors into sections of their own, since Daumier seemed to take a special delight in puncturing the pretensions of the professional men of his time. We have also reserved a special section for that dubious character, Robert Macaire, perhaps Daumier's supreme lithographic triumph. The drawings, sculpture, and paintings which follow offer only a brief glimpse of works which could well deserve their separate books. They are included here because they are necessary to an understanding and appreciation of a truly versatile artist. All of the lithographs appear with their original French captions and translations. (A catalog published in 1927 by Loys Deltiel assigned numbers to each of Daumier's lithographs. This "D" number and the year of publication appear after each translation.) In some cases the meaning of the caption may be obscure, so we have included historical explanations which appear at the end of this volume.

The editors wish to acknowledge the help of many in preparing this book. We especially wish to thank Mr. Michel Goldberg, The Joseph H. Hirshhorn Collection, Mr. George Lauscher, The National Gallery of Art, Mr. and Mrs. Robert E. Stein, The Walters Art Gallery, and Miss Stephanie Winston.

Honoré Daumier: An Appreciation

By Frank and Dorothy Getlein

Toward the end of his long life as painter and etcher, Goya, in exile at Bordeaux, made a few prints in the newly invented process of lithography. When Goya died, in 1828, a twenty-year-old Parisian, Honoré Daumier, was perfecting both a mastery of the lithograph and a social point of view admirably suited to the new print form and to the adventures of France during Daumier's lifetime.

The adventures, of course, are still going on, and not only in France. In that country, however, there has always been a certain special quality about the adventures, for it was in France that they began. The French Revolution posed an enormous threat to all authorities in all areas of life in all countries. The "adventures" in politics and economics that Daumier watched so closely and portrayed so brilliantly are generally of two kinds: the direct attempt to erase the Revolution from history and thus restore all things as they were before the deluge; and the judo-like attempt to turn the force of the Revolution to one's own ends and against the ends of liberty, equality, and fraternity. The ideal of the fathers, Péguy noted, was to die for the Republic; the ideal of the sons was to live off it.

The two adventures, and certainly the two different kinds of adventurer, went frequently together. The two were not only allied but embodied in a single person by the time Daumier was adult and aware of the France that was to be his model and his public for almost half a century. The person was Louis-Philippe, the last king of France. Napoleon himself had successfully turned the Revolution into an expression of his military genius and vulgar tastes. When his dream of reason went bankrupt, the receivers were the absolutists of Europe. They didn't much care who ruled France so long as it wasn't the French people. The last of a trio of handmade kings was Louis-Philippe. His reign coincided with the rise of a new class, the entrepreneurs, capitalists, and speculators who had made their fortunes in the chaos of the Revolution and were determined, under the revived monarchy, to expand them. Louis-Philippe, the "bourgeois king," identified himself completely with the new class and invited its members to help themselves to the public and private wealth of France. They fell to with a will.

The Revolution, however, had left another creation behind, the popular press. Large parts of the press, then as now, were for sale, but the very availability of papers for purchase by political parties or entrepreneurs at least insures the possibility of some parts of the press remaining free. To that free press the young Daumier attached himself and became the first great artist in lithography.

Senefelder's magical stone had the precise virtues needed for the popular press. Daumier drew directly on the stone, thus eliminating all the steps between drawn comment and the plate prepared for printing. Speed and directness are essential to the political and social artist and never more so than in a period of rapid change. The lithographic stone also permitted large numbers of impressions, a quality that has more than technical implications. The lithographic artist was thus in almost daily, always direct, contact with a public limited only by the appeal of the work itself. In his professional career as graphic journalist and editorialist, Daumier made some four thousand lithographs, many more drawings, and a respectable number of paintings and pieces of sculpture, all of them informed by his capacity for social indignation, by expressive line and by his eye for flaws and dangers to the France he loved.

Daumier was presented with his profession by the man who invented it, the editor Charles Philipon, whose two papers, the *Charivari* and the *Caricature,* began preparing the revolution of 1848 almost as soon as Louis-Philippe became king in 1830.

As early as 1832, Daumier made his own contribution to Philipon's war with the monarchy. *Gargantua,* named for the giant in Rabelais, shows the king as an endlessly hungry ogre, fed by assiduous ministers of state and new industrialists; in goes the gold, out come contracts and patents of nobility for stock jobbers and swindlers, as the working people are exploited to pay for the feast. The Gargantuan hunger of the new regime was not confined to the monarch himself. The throne, occupied only by the choice prizes of government, dominates a herd of the new men feeding like swine to Daumier's description of them: *Very Humble, Very Submissive, Very Obedient and Above All Very Voracious Subjects.*

Louis-Philippe, the "Pear King" as Daumier and Philipon styled him, did not take these attacks from a free press without protest. With Daumier the protest took the form of a fine of five hundred francs and six months in prison. Daumier thus began the tradition of the journalist in jail.

He continued the attack on Louis-Philippe and in the process rose to his first great achievements as journalist-printmaker. The king's dissolution of the French legislature is recorded with another line from Rabelais, *Ring Down the Curtain, the Farce is Over.* Louis-Philippe as the clown Pierrot suspends representative government. The legislature itself, "very submissive, very obedient," became the classic model for corrupt lawmakers in *The Legislative Belly.* The anatomy of the legislators, large as it is, is enlarged further in the very architecture of their chamber, seen by Daumier as row upon expanding row, each dedicated to the fat and flabby in spirit as well as body. The Marquis de Lafayette, the same soldier who played a part in the American Revolution, was, as an old man, a focus for opposition to the bourgeois king, and Daumier pictures the hypocritical grief of Louis-Philippe at Lafayette's funeral. Here, as in *Ring Down the Curtain,* the pear-shaped figure of the king passes beyond political satire of the moment and joins the gallery of human types not so much created as perceived and fixed forever by literature and art.

The actual Louis-Philippe, far from being grateful at being thus assured a place in the history of human achievement, began the inevitable encroachment of freedom of the press. Daumier warned him off by pointing to the fate of one of his predecessors, Charles X, in *Don't Meddle with the Press!* Laws against the poor seeking justice and against the press seeking truth became rapidly more severe and more severely enforced. In a police raid in a poor district of Paris, Louis-Philippe's agents murdered the family of an innocent workingman. Daumier commemorated the event in a great lithograph named for the address and the day of the police murders, *Rue Transnonain, April 15, 1834.* The stark shaft of light across the center of the picture combines the confusion of the bedclothes with the bayoneted corpse in his nightshirt. The foreshortening of the body compresses the sense of quiet outrage which is given great impetus from the almost hidden body of the child beneath the body of its father. On the right, the staring eyes of a dead old man emphasize another depth sounded by the regime. On the left, the shadows seem calm and peaceful behind the glare of massacre in the center of the picture. But in those gray grainy shadows we see the humble articles of toilet of the urban poor and on the floor the lifeless body of the woman of the house.

The straightforward realism of the portrayal contrasts sharply with the exaggerated caricature of Daumier's other political lithographs. At this point, the style says, the reign of Louis-Philippe has gone beyond parody. The representation of the facts alone is more powerful and more damaging than any comment by distortion. The event provides its own commentary.

It would be pleasant to record that these powerful blows for freedom had their intended effect. They did not. More than a dozen years later the revolution of 1848 toppled Louis-Philippe from his throne, and no doubt the work of Daumier and Philipon was a factor of some kind in the final explosion. But the immediate result of the attack was the passing of the "September Laws" making journalistic opposition illegal. *Caricature* went out of business. Philipon and Daumier directed their attention to other aspects of the brave new world of the bourgeois king. The king had made himself safe. It was the turn of the bourgeois.

There followed, over a period of two years, Daumier's first great lithographic series, the one hundred pictures of the ingenuity, roguery, and energy of Robert Macaire, the very epitome of the new men. The Macaire adventures do not constitute a consecutive story, as do, for example, the *Progresses* of Hogarth. They show, rather, the arrival in France of the promoter, Robert Macaire, and his explosion into all fields of human activity. The optimistic, fast-talking Macaire spins dreams of fortune to all who listen, and makes his own fortune out of their desire for something for nothing. He is accompanied by the skinny, down-at-the-heels Bertrand, a kind of Sancho Panza to the knight of enterprise. At their first appearance, Macaire, himself almost in rage, announces his love of "industry" and his intention to plunder the Bank of France, financiers, "all the world." Bertrand cautions, "But the police?" To which Macaire replies, in the spirit of the age, "You are an animal, Bertrand. Who would arrest a millionaire?"

That kind of one-paragraph story accompanied each of the lithographs and was written by Philipon. Yet it is no more proper to say that Daumier illustrated the writing of his friend than to say, as is said occasionally, that Daumier illustrated Balzac. Rather, Balzac and Daumier—and Philipon as well—were keenly aware of the new tone in Paris life in the thirties and forties, a tone of strident opportunism backed by ruthless manipulation of public confidence and public institutions.

When pressed by need, Macaire is capable of begging in the streets, but even then he surrounds his act with an aura of fallen grandeur, of a nobleman come on evil days; he is *Robert Macaire, the Distinguished Beggar.* And he is distinguished. He holds his hand with elegance and inflates his rags with a sense of destiny momentarily in pawn. But, even in rags, he is more at home on the platform of a hired carriage, with Bertrand beating the drum as Macaire cries his worthless shares of stock: "Ladies and gentlemen, silver mines, gold mines, diamond mines . . ." As Robert Macaire pushes his merchandise, the shares do acquire a value beyond their intrinsic value of waste paper. They represent, in the first instance, the dreams of avarice of the customers; more negotiably, they represent a created demand which is nonetheless real for being a demand for that which does not exist.

In a similar way, Robert Macaire himself takes on a certain specious reality as the series progresses. He more than half-believes his own incessant propaganda; he is wholly identified with the preposterous public figure he has created for himself. He moves confidently through swindle after swindle, examining all aspects of Parisian life for the opportunities they present to the man of enterprise. As he makes his examinations and calculates his risks, Robert Macaire improves his dress and so enhances his own reality. The tense line of that leg, the jaunty tilt of the hat, the muffler about the chin and the eager innocence of the face create a type that is with us yet.

Macaire becomes a lawyer, a doctor, a dentist, a druggist, but always and everywhere an "agent of affairs," in the French phrase that is so much more Macaire than "business agent." The telephone booth being still in the future, the streets of Paris were his office, hearth and home—somebody else's were equally his, as in *Exploitation of Love.* No human sentiment, particularly those shared by most of mankind, is foreign to Macaire's promotion, as in his touching speech at the grave of his mother. Toward the end of the series, looking at the France around him, Macaire could open his heart to Bertrand: "All the same it is flattering to have made so many disciples." Deeply sensitive to the limits of gullibility, Macaire takes his exit with grace, with sacks of money and with a touching farewell to *La Patrie,* while the practical Bertrand hurries him across the frontier. Daumier found other things to do, but Robert Macaire had lived before Daumier and easily survived him. Macaire went to America; when the Securities Exchange Commission caused his retirement from finance, he went into television, where he writes, directs, and plays all the parts in many of the entertainments and all of the commercials.

As for Daumier, he cast his eye upon the rest of Paris. The artist had begun life, when he was fourteen, as a law-court messenger and he brought his early memories up to date in a memorable series on the *Men of Justice.* "You have lost your suit, it is true," the lawyer consoles his client, "but you have had the pleasure of hearing me argue." In the figure of the defeated advocate there is, perhaps, a touch of the Macaire line, as there is in many of the Parisian types Daumier drew.

That line can even become feminine, or at least be used to show a feminine phenomenon, *Les Bas-Bleus* or *The Blue Stockings,* who were then taking over the writing of sentimental literature. Daumier showed the literary ladies moving in on libraries, press clubs and the ancient process of mutual boosting. He noted that the Blue Stockings fared forth to literary business, leaving their husbands at home as nursemaids. Like Macaire, the Blue Stockings crossed the Atlantic, where they went into the magnolia business with steady success.

In Paris, as in America, there was a great vogue for the manners and buildings of ancient Rome and Greece. The bourgeois thought to turn themselves into the gods and heroes of antiquity. Daumier reversed the process. In a series of lithographs called *Ancient History,* he portrayed the immortals and mortals of old in the bodies and faces of his contemporaries in Paris. The love of Hero and Leander, thwarted by the waters of the Hellespont, is aided by water wings. *The Night of Love* at the end of the Odyssey finds Odysseus in bed with Penelope enjoying what he had long missed: a good night's sleep. Throughout the series, the romantic and faraway is turned into the prosaic, comic, and everyday.

In 1848 Daumier had the opportunity to pay his last respects to Louis-Philippe, as the bourgeois king departed for bourgeois England and liberty returned to France. The artist noted an arrival to balance the departure, the *Napoleonic Packetboat.* Throughout the brief life of the Second Republic, France was alive with a new set of enemies of liberty, the followers of Louis Napoleon, determined to revive the empire. To depict their efforts, their characters and their style, Daumier invented a sinister figure, Ratapoil. Propagandist, political dirty worker, Ratapoil bore a distinct resemblance to Louis Napoleon. Wearing the beard and mustaches of the future emperor, dressed in seedy dignity and always carrying a cudgel, Ratapoil, in Daumier's lithographs, stalked through France. The new Napoleon was elected president of the republic; Ratapoil led demonstrations for the empire. He promised all things to all men. He skulked around the edges of the government. He created images of glory and, like Macaire, he specialized in creating a demand.

He succeeded. The republic became again an empire. Laws again were passed to control the insolence of the press and Daumier again shifted his attention to the whole spectacle of Parisian life.

Daumier noted the opening rounds of the battle that still goes on as to whether photography is art. He went to the theater and always looked more searchingly at the audience than at the stage. He went to the art gallery and ignored the pictures, watching instead the effects of Manet's *Olympia* upon the viewers and those of a critic on the artists. Throughout the middle sixties, Daumier's crayon was never still, echoing in its movements the nervous rhythm of the capital of the Second Empire. With sardonic humor, the artist staked out the classic subjects of journalist cartoonists ever since and he also ventured into territory his successors have generally stayed

clear of. Like everyone in Europe, Daumier became aware of the warlike intentions of Bismarck's Prussia. He saw, too, the use being made of war on the Paris stock exchange. In the last years before the Franco-Prussian War, Daumier drew incessantly against the coming danger. He saw the "European Equilibrium" precariously maintained on bayonets. He drew a vision of all the wars since his time in *The Dream of the Inventor of the Needle Gun,* with everybody dead except the grinning figure of the man of military science.

Daumier's warnings had never saved France before and they did not now. The empire killed itself upon the Prussian bayonets as it had killed the republic beneath the cudgels of Ratapoil. Daumier, old before his years, drew one last great political lithograph, employing, for almost the first time, the stock symbolism of poetry and rhetoric: the great oak is shattered by the storm and bent by the wind, but there is a rift in the clouds and there are fresh leaves on the single branch. *Poor France,* the title runs, *The trunk is blasted, but the roots still hold!*

All his life Honoré Daumier fought a losing battle for the republic. All his life he worked hard, sometimes having as many as eight lithographic stones at once laid out around a table. All his life he studied mankind and, with brilliant crayon, tried to get mankind to join him in this study. Daumier was devoted to industry, to freedom, to honesty. In addition, he was a genius. In his last years the artist reaped the reward of these virtues, namely, poverty. In the first years of the Third Republic, which preserved and gave new impetus to many of the character traits of the last kingdom and the Second Empire. Daumier found himself destitute. Through the kindness of an artist friend, Daumier was given a roof over his head for his last few years.

The whole period of his life and the period since his death have both been great ones for artists coming down from Mount Sinai with the single definitive word on what must be done in art. Daumier never ascended Sinai, or, if he did, he kept quiet about any universal laws entrusted to his care. He did say one thing, but it is such a general statement that it could apply to all trades. Yet, it is personal enough to stand as the artist's word on his work. In a dedication to a friend, Daumier once wrote, simply, "It is necessary to be of one's time."

The Lithographs

Daumier's earliest lithographs are signed H.D. and show Parisian National Guardsmen. They are dated September 13, 1822. Daumier was only fourteen years old at the time, but we can be fairly sure of the date of these and subsequent lithographs since a compulsory act, the *Dépôt Légal,* required all printed matter to be submitted for approval and retained for reference by the government.

The next Daumier prints registered appear in 1830. These deal with the July revolution and insult Talleyrand and Louis-Philippe. In 1830, Charles Philipon founded *La Caricature* with this opening statement: *"Caricature* appearing only weekly, must and will be a highly finished production; its illustrations carefully executed and printed on good rag paper, make it a periodical for collectors and bibliophiles." He intended to have two lithographs and one sheet of copy in every issue.

In 1831, *Caricature* printed the famous Gargantua cartoon insulting Louis-Philippe, and Daumier was sent to prison from September, 1832, to January, 1833, for this act of *lèse majesté.* Most of the pictures in *La Caricature* were small, with countless tiny figures. Daumier's style was different, and he gradually influenced the other contributors. He drew clear and simple designs, some with only a single large figure. Daumier's contributions increased each year until 1835, when *Caricature* ceased publication.

In 1832, Philipon founded a second journal. "For the benefit of cafés and those friends of the graphic arts who prefer variety to political spice, we are creating a daily which will bring a new sketch every morning and which, being printed more rapidly than *Caricature* and with less finished drawings, is going to be sold at a price otherwise reserved for so-called 'literary' periodicals." This was the famous *Charivari,* which lasted well into the twentieth century. *Charivari* means "derisive serenade." At the beginning of their association, there was no difference in Daumier's contributions to *Charivari* and *Caricature.* Both journals printed political lithographs, but *Charivari* was more adaptable to the restrictive press laws that were put into effect in 1835. Now, instead of kings and ministers, the bourgeoisie began to make their appearance, and Daumier's political rapier was sheathed.

Whenever the absolutist pressure was relaxed or removed, Daumier attacked the regime. These outbursts were very brief, however, since the government would clamp down on the paper almost immediately. *Charivari* and Daumier formed a lifetime partnership, and it was this paper that supported him for most of his life. He had 90 pictures published in *Caricature,* but his output for *Charivari* was a staggering 3,300 published lithographs.

The pictures were almost all drawn with soft black chalk on yellowish slate. Where the stone absorbed the chalk it also sucked up the black printer's ink, transferring it in the press to rolls of paper. Sometimes Daumier drew with a pen on the stone, and this permitted a more delicate line and finer detail.

In his early lithographs, Daumier's style was almost a reproduction of his sculpture. Gradually it becomes more free with silhouettes and greater use of backgrounds. Movement is suggested by outlines, and shading becomes increasingly more important.

Daumier refined his style constantly, and we now recognize him as one of the greatest lithographic artists of all time. The plates that follow are a brief selection showing many of the facets of his art, but no selection can cover everything he accomplished. Each individual picture is either delightful or moving, but his work as a whole is one of the great gifts we have received from the world of art.

Passe ton chemin, cochon!

"On your way, pig!"   (D. 1—1830)

Il a raison l'moutard—Eh oui, c'est nous qu'a fait la révolution et c'est eux qui la mangent . . . (la galette).

"He's right, that fellow—it is we who made the revolution, and it is they who are eating the cake." (D. 8—1830)

CH. DE LAM....

CHARLES DE LAMETH.   (D. 43—1832)

Ksssse! Pédro . . . Kssse! Kssse! Miguel! Ces deux capons-là ne se feront jamais grand mal.

"Pssst! Pedro . . . Pssst! Pssst! Miguel! These two gutless wonders will never really fight. They might get hurt." (D. 61—1833)

A da-da sur mon bidet . . . (Romance enfantine.)

"Giddyap, horsie . . ." (Children's song.)   (D. 179—1833)

M. GUÌZ . . .

Mr. Guiz . . .   (D. 74—1833)

L'IVROGNE.

The Drunkard. (D. 189—1834)

LE VENTRE LÉGISLATIF

Aspect des bancs ministériels de la chambre impr...

Chez Aubert, galerie véro dodat.

The Legislative Body

View of the ministerial benches of the virtuous Chamber of 1834. (D. 131—1834)

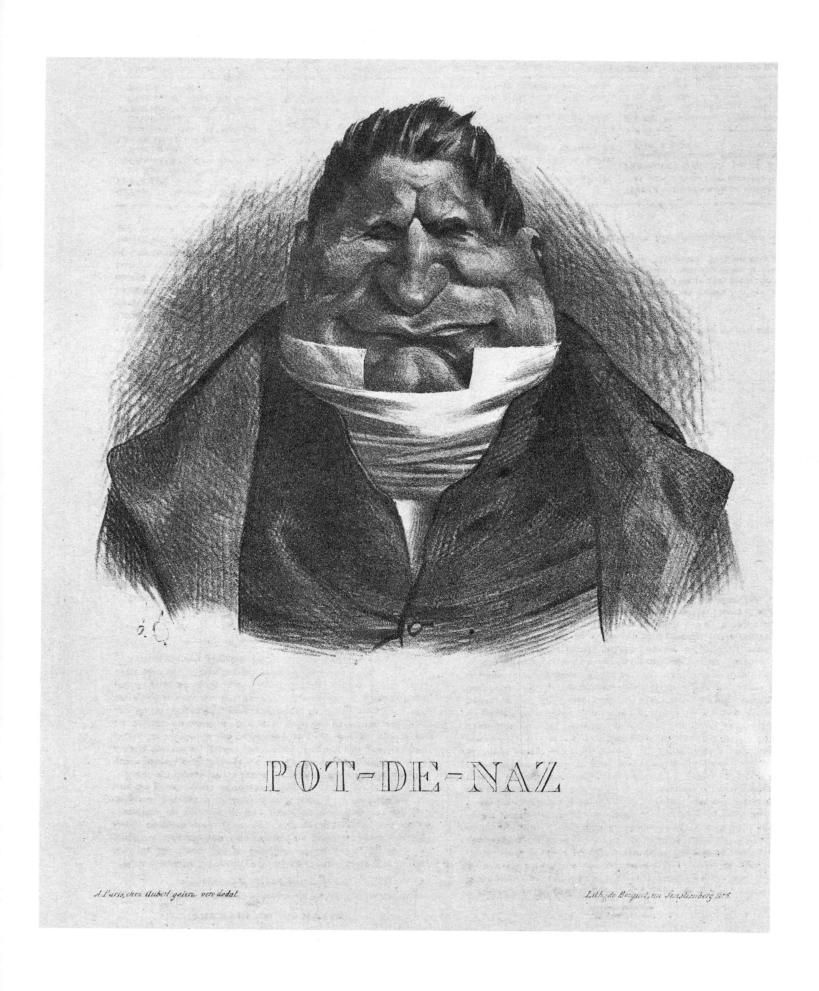

POT-DE-NAZ

A Paris, chez Aubert galerie vero dodat

Lith. de Becquet, rue Furstemberg N°6

MR. POT-DE-NAZ. (D. 152—1833)

Ne vous y frottez pas!

"Don't tangle with him!"   (D. 133—1834)

Enfoncé La Fayette! . . . Attrape, mon vieux!

"Now that Lafayette is dead! . . . it's your turn."   (D. 134—1834)

Rue Transnonain, le 15 avril 1834.

Transnonain Street, April 15, 1834.   (D. 135—1834)

13

H.D.

14

Celui-là, on peut le mettre en liberté! Il n'est pas dangereux.

"Oh well, we can let this one go. He's not dangerous." (D. 85—1834)

Un rentier des bons royaux—Un rentier des Cortès.

Two Spanish Creditors.   (D. 87—1834)

THE MODERN GALILEO.   And time passes anyway.   (D. 93—1834)

16

Petits! petits! petits! . . . venez! venez! venez! . . . venez donc, Dindons!

"Here chick, chick, chick, . . . Come, come, come! . . . Come on then, turkeys!"   (D. 97—1834)

Juges des Accusés d'avril. Mr. Barbé-Marbois.

One of the judges of the defendants of April—Mr. Barbé-Marbois. (D. 117—1835)

Mr. Chose, the best rope walker in Europe. (D. 161—1833)

SOUVENIR DE S⸍ PÉLAGIE.

Paris, chez Aubert, Galerie vero dodat   Lith. de Benard, rue de l'Abbaye 4

Souvenir of St. Pélagie.   (D. 192—1834)

LE PETIT CLERC.

Le petit clerc mange peu, court beaucoup, flâne davantage et revient le plus tard possible à l'étude où il est le souffre-douleur. Il s'appelle ordinairement Pitou, Godard ou Galuchet.

FRENCH TYPES.

THE CLERK.

The minor clerk eats little, runs much, loiters about as much as possible, returns as late as he can to the office where he serves as whipping boy. His name is usually Pitou, Godard, or Galuchet. (D. 260—1835)

UN QUIPROQUO.

Vous vous trompez, vous vous trompez! Allez-vous-en au diable sacrebleu! . . . Ah! c'est pas vous qu'êtes mort? excusez.

A MISUNDERSTANDING.

"You're wrong, you're making a mistake! Go to the devil, for God's sake!"
"Oh, you mean you are not the dead man? Excuse, please."   (D. 537—1838)

NEUF HEURES DU SOIR.

M. Coquelet éteignant sa lumière termine une journée qui semblable à la veille et semblable au lendemain retrace la peinture exacte de la vie du célibataire!

THE DAY OF A BACHELOR.

9 P.M.

Mr. Coquelet, on extinguishing his light, ends a day exactly like the one before and like the one tomorrow. (D. 618—1839)

LES SALTIMBANQUES.

Vous voyez ici les grandes célébrités de la France littéraire, musicale et artistique, ils ont tous 36 pieds au-dessous du niveau de la mer. . . .

THE CHARLATANS.

"You see here the great figures of literary, musical, and artistic France, they are all 36 feet below sea level. . . ."
(D. 620—1839)

UNE *VICTIME DES FACTIONS.*

Ha . . . a . . . at . . . stchutz!! allons bon, v'la mon nez qui pleut aussi. Décidément M. Jacqueminot devrait dresser des canards pour monter la garde par ce temps-ci . . . et encore ha . . . a . . . at . . . stchutz! ils s'enrhumeraient.

PARISIAN EMOTIONS.

A VICTIM OF PARTY STRIFE.

Accchhhoooo! Oh well, my nose is raining too. Mr. Jacqueminot ought to train ducks to stand guard in weather like this . . . but still . . . accchhhoooo! . . . they'd catch pneumonia too. (D. 728—1842)

Ma foi je ne sais pas comment ils étaient à Austerlitz, mais ça ne pouvait guère être mieux.

COQUETRY.

Goodness me, I don't know how they looked at Austerlitz, but it could hardly have been better than this.
(D. 742—1840)

Ce matin avant l'aurore,   *De ton Papa c'est la Fête,*
Un Dieu vint me réveiller;   *Fais-lui quelque don flatteur*
Il me dit: tu dors encore.   *En lui posant sure la tête*
Est-il temps de sommeiller?   *Une couronne de fleurs.*

WEDDED LIFE.

This morning before dawn,   Today is your Papa's birthday,
A god came to awake me.   Make him a flattering gift
He said to me: You are   By placing on his head
   still sleeping. A crown of flowers.
Is it still time to sleep?   (D. 627—1839)

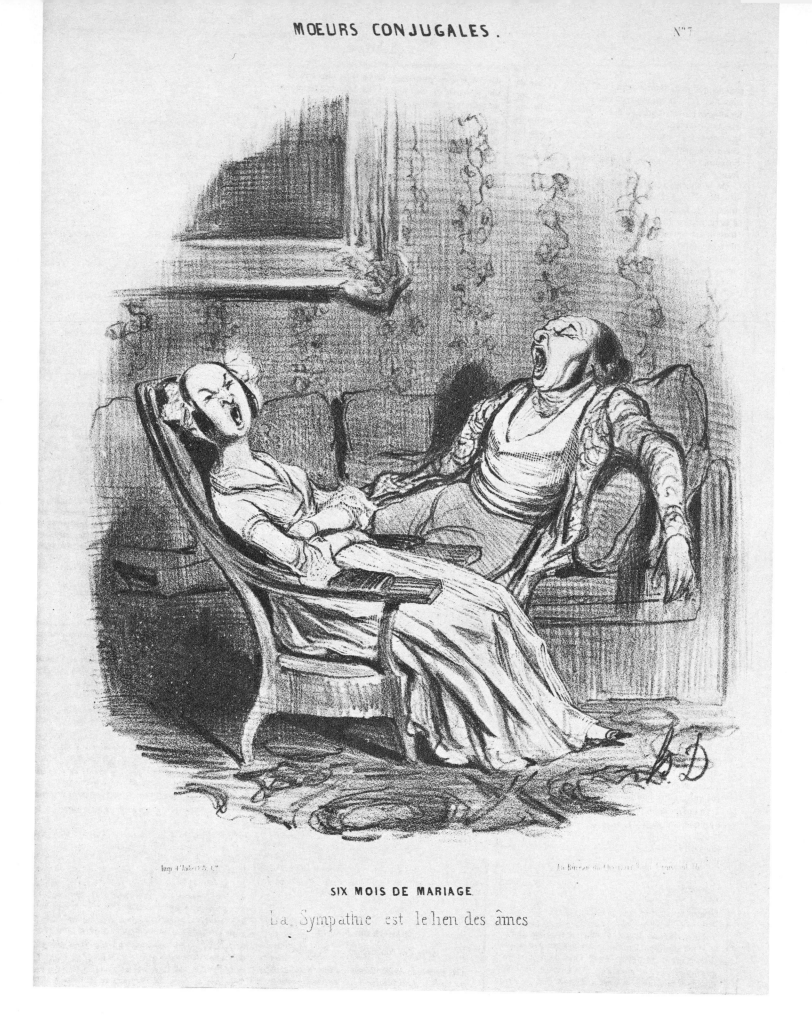

SIX MOIS DE MARIAGE.

La Sympathie est le lien des âmes

WEDDED LIFE.

SIX MONTHS OF MARRIAGE.

Sympathy is the bond of souls. (D. 630—1839)

Le danger des passions où souvent l'on se trouve entraîné plus loin qu'on ne voudrait.

FISHING.

The danger of the passions is that one often finds oneself carried farther along than one wishes to go. (D. 820—1840)

LE MEMBRE DE TOUTES LES ACADEMIES.

Diable de discours; impossibilité de retenir . . . ah! j'y suis, Messieurs, c'est avec émotion que je viens donner à l'Europe **des preuves d'un savoir** *. . . qui pourrait être plus étendu . . . mais si je n'en sais pas davantage, c'est par modestie! La séance d'aujourd'hui sera consacrée aux bouchons de liège . . . cette question si futile au point de vue ordinaire; et si intéressante pour l'humanité; nous examinerons ensuite l'influence des pains à cacheter sur la litterature . . . j'aurai ensuite l'honneur de vous faire entendre un rapport lumineux sur les allumettes chimiques. (Séance du 20 janvier 1942)*

BOHEMIANS OF PARIS.
A MEMBER OF EVERY ACADEMY.

A devil of a speech, impossible to remember it. Oh, I have it: "Gentlemen, it is with full heart that I come to give all of Europe the fruits of my knowledge . . . this bit could be longer . . . and if I seem not to know enough, mark it down to my modesty. Today's meeting will be devoted to cork bottle stoppers. . . . this question so useless from an ordinary point of view; and so interesting for humanity; we will then examine the influence of post marks on literature. . . . I will then have the honor of presenting to you a glowing report on sulphur matches." (Meeting of January 20, 1942)   (D. 846—1842)

"Une des curiosités de Francfort qui disparaîtra bientôt j'en ai peur, c'est la boucherie, il est impossible de voir un plus splendide amas de chair fraîche. Les bouchers sanglants et les bouchères roses causent avec grâce sous des guirlandes de gigots. Un ruisseau rouge dont deux fontaines jaillissantes modifient à peine la couleur, coule et fume au milieu de la rue!"

A GREAT POET REMINISCES ABOUT HIS JOURNEY.

"One of the curiosities of Frankfurt (which will, I'm afraid, disappear one day) is the slaughterhouse. One could never see a more splendid mass of fresh flesh. The bloody butchers and their wives chat gracefully under garlands of guts. A red stream, whose two gushing fountains add to the color, runs and steams in the middle of the street!" (*Le Rhin* by Victor Hugo) (D. 982—1842)

Oui, monsieur, j'ai mis ma vie politique à nu devant le pays. Je croyais alors que mon amour sincère pour nos institutions me rendait digne de représenter mes concitoyens . . . Je me suis trompé, monsieur, grossièrement trompé!!!

A PROFESSION OF FAITH.

"Yes, monsieur, I have bared my political life before the country. I believed then that my sincere love for our institutions made me worthy of representing my fellow-citizens. . . . I was mistaken, sir, grossly mistaken!"
(D. 783—1842)

TRAGIC-CLASSICAL PHYSIOGNOMIES.

"Yes, I will come to his temple to worship the Eternal." D. 895—1842)
(*Athalie*)

UN ABUS DE CONFIANCE.

Les misérables!!! Voler un procureur du roi, qui nage sous la sauve-garde des lois naturelles et sociales! sans mon chapeau, je rentrais nu chez moi; dans quel temps vivons-nous!

THE BATHERS.

A BETRAYAL OF CONFIDENCE.

The scoundrels! To steal from the king's man who was swimming beneath the protection of all natural and social laws! If it were not that I still have my hat, I would be returning home naked. What times we live in! (D. 788—1842)

ALEXANDRE ET DIOGÈNE.

Le Sage qui goipait dans le simple appareil
D'un voyou fumant sa bouffarde.
Dit au héros qui le regarde:
Esbigne-toi de mon soleil!

Goualante de Mr Eugène Sue.

ANCIENT HISTORY.   ALEXANDER AND DIOGENES.

Lounging in the simple attire of a tramp,
The wise man, puffing at his pipe,
Said to the hero, looking at him:
"Be off, out of my sun."   (D. 944—1842)

ANCIENT HISTORY

L'EDUCATION D'ACHILLE.

L'inflexible Chiron fesait chaque matin
Endéver bien souvent son élève mutin.
Las! que de professeurs rompent nos jeunes têtes;
Et sans être sans torts, sont plus qu'à moitié bêtes!

THE EDUCATION OF ACHILLES.

The iron-willed Chiron angered each morning
His most rebellious pupil.
Alas! So many teachers crack our young heads,
And without having remorse, they drive us half mad.
(D. 933—1842)

LES ÉCURIES D'AUGIAS.

Se faire recureur, pour un héros superbe,
C'est, par Hercule, un goût difficile à chanter.
Mais comme le dit un proverbe:
D'écours et des couleurs on ne peut disputer.

Calembourg inédit de Mr Delessert

ANCIENT HISTORY.   THE AUGEAN STABLES.

That a magnificent hero voluntarily becomes a stable boy,
That—by Hercules—is a taste difficult to be lyrical about,
But in the words of a proverb:
There is no accounting for taste.   (D. 950—1842)

Chez Bauger R. du Croissant, 16.　　　　Imp d'Aubert & Cie.

CLÉMENCE DE MINOS

Heureux le pâle humain, qui, dans ce noir refuge
Arrive quand Minos lit son **Charivari**;
Il est sûr d'être absous, car on sait que tout juge.
Est désarmé lorsqu'il a ri.

(Petite réclame poétique)

ANCIENT HISTORY.

THE CLEMENCY OF MINOS.

Fortunate indeed is the pale human being, in this black refuge,
Who arrives at the moment when Minos is reading his copy
　　of *Charivari*;
He is certain to receive absolution, for—as every one knows—
Any judge is disarmed as soon as he laughs.　(D. 974—1843)

ANCIENT HISTORY.

LE BEAU NARCISSE.	THE BEAUTIFUL NARCISSUS.
Il était jeune et beau, de leurs douches haleines, *Les zéphirs caressaient ses contours pleins d'attraits,* *Et dans le miroir des fontaines* *Il aimait comme nous à contempler ses traits.* *(Quatrain intime de M. Marcisse de Salvandy.)*	He was young and beautiful, with sweet breath, The breezes caressed his lovely contours, And in the mirror of the fountains, He loved to gaze upon his features. (Intimate quatrain of Mr. Narcissus of Salvandy.) (D. 947—1842)

ANCIENT HISTORY.

LA CHUTE D'ICARE.

Tandis que le soleil lui rôtissait les ailes,
Son vieux gredin de père, auteur de ce moyen,
Disait, le voyant choir des voûtes éternelles:
Décidément ça ne vaut rien.
(Un poètre qui ne va qu'en fiacre.)

THE FALL OF ICARUS.

While the sun roasted his wings,
His old bastard of a father, the instigator of these proceedings,
Said, on seeing him fall from the eternal canopy,
Decidedly, this isn't any good.
(By a poet who only travels in horse-drawn hansoms.)

(D. 955—1842)

APELLES ET CAMPASTE.

Sachant que pour son tendre et ravissant modèle
Apelles se mourait de désirs insensés,
Alexandre en grand roi lui céda cette belle
Dont il avait du reste assez.
(De l'art antique, essai poétique de M. Cavé)

ANCIENT HISTORY.

APELLES AND CAMPASTE.

Knowing that for her tender and ravishing figure
Apelles was dying from violent desire,
The great Alexander granted him that lovely one
Of whom there was plenty left.   (D. 960—1842)

L'ELECTION.

Enfoncé!!!—Ah! mes amis . . . mes bons amis, ce soir est le plus beau jour de ma vie! . . .

PARLIAMENTARY SCENES.

THE ELECTION.

"Defeated! Ah, my friends . . . my good friends, this evening is the most beautiful of my life!"   (D. 1019—1843)

Dites donc, père Loustalot . . . faut avouer que c'est un peu ennuyeux de voir comme ça toute la journée nos bras transformés en enseignes! . . . —N'm'en barlez bas! . . . avec ça que je suis enrubé du cerbeau! v'là drois quarts d'heure que j'ai enbie de me boucher le nez . . . mais j'ose pas, ça pourrait compromettre la sûreté d'un convoi . . . le premier voyageur que je verrai passer je le prierai de me rendre ce service.

THE RAILROADS.

"The truth is, old father Loustalot, that it gets very tiring to have our arms used as signals."
"Don't speak to me! I've had to blow my nose for the last hour. But I can't, the safety of the next train depends on me. The next person that comes by, I'll ask him to render me that service." (D. 1045—1843)

· Oh!.... Papa!.....

RED LETTER DAYS.

"Oh! . . . Papa!" (D. 1091—1844)

CHINESE TRIP.
CHINESE WARRIORS.

GUERRIERS CHINOIS.

Tous les Chinois ont le droit de porter, six ou huit fois par an, un fusil, une giberne et même un bonnet à poil: alors ils se livrent, plus ou moins volontiers à des patrouilles nocturnes qui ont pour but de maintenir la tranquillité publique. Seulement il arrive assez souvent que le chef nommé Ka-Po-Ral a infiniment de peine à empêcher ses guerriers de chanter à gorge déployée: "la mère Go-Di-Chon" ou autres romances chinoises, et c'est en se réveillant en sursaut que les bons bourgeois apprennent qu'on veille sur leur repos.

Each Chinese man has the right to carry, six or eight times a year, a gun, a cartridge pouch, and even a bearskin hat: then he goes, more or less willingly, on the night patrols for the maintenance of public order. Unfortunately, it frequently happens that the commander of the force, Ka-Po-Ral, often has some difficulty in preventing his men from singing at the top of their lungs, "Old Mother Go-Di-Chon" or other Chinese ditties. But when the solid burgher wakes with a jump, he knows that his rest is being protected by the guardians of the peace. (D. 1207—1844)

*Allons! . . . on n'a pas encore rendu compte de mon roman aujourd'hui! ces journalistes s'occupent maintenant tous
les matins des Lièvres . . . des Perdreaux . . . des Bécasses! . . . et ils ne pensent pas à moi . . . c'est inconcevable! . . .*

THE BLUESTOCKINGS.

Oh my, they still haven't reviewed my novel today! Every day these critics review the Lièvres, the Perdreaux,
the Bécasses, and they ignore my work. It's disgraceful! (D. 1230—1844)

LE PARTERRE DE L'ODEON.

L'auteur! . . . l'auteur! . . . l'auteur! . . . —Messieurs, votre impatience va être satisfaite . . . vous désirez connaître l'auteur de l'ouvrage remarquable qui vient d'obtenir un si grand, et je dois le dire, si légitime succès . . . cet auteur . . . c'est môa! . . .

THE BLUESTOCKINGS.

A BOX AT THE THEATRE ODEON.

"Author, author, author!"

"Gentlemen, your eagerness shall be satisfied. You wish to know the author of the remarkable work that has just won such a great and—if I may say so—such a deserved success. It is I!"   (D. 1237—1844)

Nos comptes sont faciles à établir . . . vous m'aviez confié mille exemplaires de votre recueil poétique intitulé "soupirs de mon âme," vingt-sept volumes ont été donnés aux journaux . . . et en défalquant ce que j'ai vendu, je trouve qu'il me reste juste neuf cent soixante-treize "soupirs de votre âme" dans mon magasin! . . .

THE BLUESTOCKINGS.

"We can settle our accounts very simply. You left with me one thousand copies of your poetic anthology entitled 'Sighs of My Soul,' twenty-seven copies were given to the press . . . and on checking the rate of sale, I find that I have only 973 'Sighs of Your Soul' left in my store!" (D. 1250—1844)

THE CON MEN.

THE ELECTION GAME.

LA CAROTTE DE L'ELECTION.

Mon cher ami, ne croyez pas que je vienne vous demander votre voix, je respecte trop l'indépendance des opinions; c'est madame la baronne qui m'a dit: Allez voir ce pauvre Galuzot; dites à sa petite femme qu'elle me néglige; que je lui en veux, informez-vous de leurs délicieux enfants et dites que je veux absolument les avoir à diner.

"My dear friend, please don't think that I come to ask you for your vote; I respect too much the independence of your opinions. In fact, I am here to convey the regards of Madame the Baroness. She said to me, 'Go see the poor Galuzot; tell his little wife that she is neglecting me; inquire as to the health of their lovely children, and tell them that I must have them to dinner very soon.'" (D. 1261—1844)

THE CON MEN.

CAROTTE DRAMATIQUE. (*Couplet au public.*)

THE DRAMA GAME.

AIR DE LA SENTINELLE.

THE SENTRY'S AIR (Couplet for the public.)

A vous, messieurs, je m'adresse ce soir,
Vous avez tant d'esprit, tant de finesse;
A vous, messieurs, notre orgueil, notre espoir,
Je viens ici confesser ma faiblesse;
Ah, donnez-moi, juge trop indulgent,
Un bouclier contre bien des attaques;
Donnez-moi, public obligeant,
Vos soins, vos conseils . . . votre argent,
Et surtout donnez-moi des claques.

To you, gentlemen, I speak this evening,
You have so much spirit, so much polish;
For you, gentlemen, our pride, our hope,
I come here to bare my weakness;
Ah, give me, my too indulgent judge,
A shield against all attacks;
Give me, kindly public,
Your attention, your counsels . . . your money,
And above all, give me your claques."   (D. 1265—1844)

STRANGERS IN PARIS.

L'INDISPENSABLE VISITE CHEZ LE TAILLEUR DU PALAIS-ROYAL.

Ce paletot semble avoir été fait exprès pour monsieur . . . il lui va comme un gant! . . . —Comme un gant un peu large il me semble . . . enfin n'importe! je le garde, du moment où vous m'assurez que vous habillerez aînsi tous les membres du Club des Jockeys! . . .

THE INDISPENSABLE VISIT TO THE TAILOR OF THE PALAIS-ROYAL.

"This topcoat seems to have been made expressly for you, sir, it fits you like a glove."
"Like a very large glove, I think; oh well, it doesn't matter. I promise to take it, as soon as you promise me that you will clothe all the members of the Jockey Club like this."
(D. 1273—1844)

LES BAS BLEUS.

Chez Aubert, Pl. de la Bourse, 29.

Imp. d'Aubert & Cie.

Comment! encore une caricature sur nous, ce matin, dans le **Charivari**!... ah! jour de ma vie! j'espère bien que cette fois c'est la dernière!... et si jamais ce Daumier me tombe sous la main, il lui en coutera cher pour s'être permis de tricoter des **Bas bleus**.

THE BLUESTOCKINGS.

"What! Yet another caricature about us, in this morning's *Charivari*! Upon my soul, I hope this time it's the last one and if I should ever meet this Daumier, he'll pay dearly for having picked a hole in the Bluestockings." (D. 1259—1844)

PASTORAL SCENES.

Vas-tu te taire avec tes cocoricos . . . c'est bien la peine de venir à la campagne pour dormir tranquillement. —Je suis tous les jours réveillé à trois heures du matin . . . je dormais encore mieux à Paris même du vivant de ma femme! . . .

"Oh, shut up with those cock-a-doodle-do's! I come to the country for a little peace, and you wake me up every morning at 3 A.M.! I slept better in Paris, even when my wife was alive!"   (D. 1421—1845)

Un jeune homme qui est l'espoir et l'orgueil de la famille Badinguet.

THE MIDDLE CLASS.

The young man who is the hope and pride of the Badinguet family. (D. 1492—1846)

Trois heures du matin, il s'apprête à aller goûter le plaisir de la chasse.

THE MIDDLE CLASS.

Three o'clock in the morning, he is getting ready to taste the joys of the hunt.   (D. 1515—1847)

THE MIDDLE CLASS.

Plus souvent que tu m'attraperas encore à satisfaire ta fantaisie d'aller dîner sur l'herbe . . . v'là deux heures que nous marchons et nous n'avons pas encore trouvé le moindre gazon . . . si j'avais su, j'aurais fourré au fond du panier notre grand tapis vert . . .

"Once again you have snared me into satisfying your fantasy of going to eat on the grass. So far, we've been walking for two hours, and the landscape has been devoid of the slightest lawn. If I had known, I would have put our large green carpet at the bottom of the basket." (D. 1519—1847)

THE MIDDLE CLASS.

Position réputée la plus commode pour avoir un joli portrait au daguerréotype.

Position reputed to be the most comfortable for an admirable daguerreotype.   (D. 1525—1847)

N'approche pas la mêche de la lumière! . . . il va peutêtre faire explosion! . . .

THE MIDDLE CLASS.

"Don't bring the light wick any closer! It could explode!" (D. 1537—1847)

UN VERITABLE AMATEUR.

THE MIDDLE CLASS.

A TRUE LOVER OF THE ARTS.   (D. 1542—1847)

THE MIDDLE CLASS.

Nous ne partirons donc pas! . . . Hortense, je crois que ça va mordre . . . rien plus qu'une petite demi-heure! . . .

"No, we will not leave! Hortense, I'm sure I feel a bite! Just a half hour more!" (D. 1549—1847)

Un fils modèle.

THE FATHERS.

A MODEL SON. (D. 1584—1847)

Inconvénient de mettre son logement à louer au mois de janvier.

LODGERS AND LANDLORDS.

"It's inconvenient to have to rent the rooms during January."   (D. 1594—1847)

Est-il dieu permis . . . Fendre du bois dans ma salle à manger! . . . Ce n'est pas un artiste à qui j'ai loué, c'est à un bûcheron! . . .

LODGERS AND LANDLORDS.

"Oh my God, chopping wood in my dining room! It wasn't an artist I rented to, it's a lumberjack!"   (D. 1596—1847)

Un locataire qui doit trois termes.

LODGERS AND LANDLORDS.

Three months behind in the rent. (D. 1613—1847)

Chez Aubert & Cⁱᵉ Pl. de la Bourse, 29.

Imp. Aubert & Cⁱᵉ

« Le spectacle est une chose bonne pour le peuple de Paris, il vient s'y délasser le soir des fatigues de la journée. »

(*Tous les moralistes.*)

AS YOU LIKE IT.

Entertainment is a good thing for the people of Paris, they come here in the evening to relax from the fatigues of the day.   (D. 1679—1849)

Chez Aubert & Cⁱᵉ Pl. de la Bourse, 29.

Imp. Aubert & Cⁱᵉ

C'est pourtant là que j'ai gravé mon chiffre amoureux . . . tiens comme il a remonté . . . moi j'ai bien baissé depuis ! . . .

AS YOU LIKE IT.

And it was there that I carved my initials of love. How high it has grown. As for me, I've slumped since then. (D. 1681—1849)

Chez Aubert. & C.ⁱᵉ Pl. de la Bourse. 29.

Imp. Aubert. & Cⁱᵉ

_ Ce n'est pas sous l'Empire qu'on aurait dansé comme ça !...

AS YOU LIKE IT.

"Under the Empire one wouldn't have danced like that."   (D. 1680—1849)

Voilà une femme qui, à l'heure solennelle où nous sommes s'occupe bêtement de ses enfants . . . qu'il y a encore en France des êtres abruptes et arriérés!

THE DIVORCEES.

"There is a woman who has nothing more important to do during these difficult times than take care of her children . . . It's no wonder France is behind the times." (D. 1770—1848)

LE GAMIN DE PARIS AUX TUILERIES.

- Cristi !..... comme on s'enfonce là dedans.

THE URCHIN OF PARIS IN THE TUILERIES.

"Christ . . . how easily you can sink in." (D. 1743—1848)

Dernier conseil des ex ministres.

LAST CABINET MEETING OF THE EX-MINISTERS.. (D. 1746—1848)

M.M. Victor Hugo et Emile Girardin cherchent a élever le prince Louis sur un pavois, ça n'est pas très solide !

ACTUALITIES.

Messrs. Victor Hugo and Emile Girardin would like to raise Prince Louis [Napoleon] on a shield which is not quite balanced. (D. 1756—1848)

Le Constitutionnel se mettant héroiquement à la tête du corps franc recruté rue de Valois et rue de Poitiers pour soutenir la cause du Prince Louis.

THE NAPOLEONIC CONSTITUTIONAL.

The Constitutional heroically places itself in the vanguard finding recruits for the cause of Prince Louis [Napoleon]. (D. 1733—1848)

Le Constitutionnel Contemplant l'Horizon Politique.

ACTUALITIES.

The Constitutional Contemplating the Political Horizon.   (D. 1909—1849)

ACTUALITES.

LE NOUVEAU ST-SEBASTIEN, VIERGE ET MARTYR.

THE NEW ST. SEBASTIAN, VIRGIN AND MARTYR.   (D. 1917—1849)

ACTUALITIES.

74

Les augures de l'Empire s'apprêtent à consulter les entrailles des canards sacrés avant que César ne choisisse d'autres ministres.

ACTUALITIES.

The soothsayers of the Empire make preparation to consult the entrails of the sacred ducks before Caesar chooses any more ministers.   (D. 1996—1850)

UN PARRICIDE.

ACTUALITIES.

A PARRICIDE.   (D. 2002—1850)

ACTUALITIES.

Eh bien, monsieur le marquis de Guizot, avouez que nous avons eu une heureuse idée d'inventer la fusion . . . il n'y a que cela qui peut sauver la France! . . . Maintenant il s'agit de nous montrer en public dans notre nouveau costume pour faire revenir les Parisiens aux anciennes, nobles et saines traditions de la culotte courte et des ailes de pigeon! . . .

"Well, Sir Marquis de Guizot, it was a happy idea indeed to invent fusion. This is the only thing that can save France! . . . Now, the thing to do is to make an appearance in public in our new costumes, and teach Parisians to return to the ancient, noble and wholesome traditions of the short culotte and the pigeon wings."　(D. 2115—1851)

RATAPOIL FESANT DE LA PROPAGANDE.

Si vous aimez votre femme, votre maison, votre champ, votre génisse et votre veau, signez, vous n'avez pas une minute à perdre! . . .

ACTUALITIES.

RATAPOIL MAKES PROPAGANDA.

"If you love your wife, your home, your friends, your heifer and your calf, sign, you don't have a minute to lose!" (D. 2117—1851)

Docteur, je vous assure que je ne suis pas aussi malade que vous me le dites! . . .

ACTUALITIES.

"Doctor, I assure you that I'm not as sick as you say I am!"   (D. 2131—1851)

UN BONAPARTISTE NOUVELLEMENT CONVERTI.

Dieu ai-je aimé cet être-là . . . je l'ai pourtant abandonné . . . il le fââlait! . . .

ACTUALITIES.

A NEWLY CONVERTED BONAPARTIST.

God knows, I loved that person! Still, I deserted him . . . I had to.   (D. 2140—1851)

L'orchestre pendant qu'on joue une tragédie.

MUSICAL SKETCHES.

View of the orchestra, during the performance of a tragedy.   (D. 2243—1852)

ACTUALITES.

Des Dames d'un demi-monde mais n'ayant pas de demi-jupes.

Middle-class women, with high-class skirts.   (D. 2624—1855)

ACTUALITIES.

L'EXPOSITION UNIVERSELLE.

AUX CHAMPS-ELYSEES.

De trois heures à six heures, grande exposition de nouveaux jupons-ballons.

UNIVERSAL EXHIBITION.   ON THE CHAMPS-ELYSEES.

From three to six, there will be a grand exhibition of new balloon-skirts. (D. 2676—1855)

A NAPLES, DELEGUES DE LA COMMISSION DES BASTONNADES

DANS L'EXERCICE DE LEURS DELICATES FONCTIONS.

Il a eu bien de la peine celui-là, à se décider à crier: VIVE LE ROI . . . mais enfin nous en sommes venus à bout . . . le voilà maintenant complètement rallié au gouvernement! . . .

ACTUALITIES.

NAPLES. DELEGATES OF THE COMMISSION OF BASTONNADES IN THE

EXERCISE OF THEIR DELICATE FUNCTIONS.

"He had a lot of trouble, that one, before he got around to saying LONG LIVE THE KING! But all's well that ends well . . . here he is now, completely bound to the government." (D. 2632—1855)

Une loge au théâtre VENTADOUR *pendant la représentation d'une tragédie italienne.*

ACTUALITIES.

A box at the Ventadour Theatre during the performance of an Italian tragedy.   (D. 2764—1856)

Faisant son apprentissage au tourniquet de la Bourse pour être cantonnier d'un chemin de fer russe.

PARISIAN SKETCHES.

At the turnstile to the Stock Exchange, serving his apprenticeship as roadmender on a Russian railroad. (D. 2919—1857)

Croyant l'apercevoir.

THE COMET OF 1857.

They think they see it. (D. 2934—1857)

L'EXPOSITION DE 1859.

Ils m'one refusé ça . . . les ignares!!

THE EXPOSITION OF 1859.

"They refused to let me show this . . . the ignoramuses!! (D. 3135—1859)

Une discussion littéraire à la deuxième Galerie.

THEATRE SKETCHES by Daumier.

A literary discussion in the second balcony.   (D. 3264—1864)

M^{on} Martinet, 172, r. Rivoli et 41, r. Vivienne   Lith Destouches, 28, r Paradis P^{se}

_ On dit que les Parisiens sont difficiles à satisfaire, sur ces quatre banquettes pas un mécon_
tent _ il est vrai que tous ces Français sont des Romains.

THEATRE SKETCHES by Daumier.

They say that it is difficult to satisfy the Parisians. In those four rows there is not one who is dissatisfied, but of course all those Frenchmen are Romans.   (D. 3263—1864)

Le rêve de l'inventeur du fusil à aiguille le jour de la Troussaint.

ACTUALITIES.

The All Saints' Day reverie of the inventor of the needle gun.   (D. 3535—1866)

LA DAME DES OEUFS.

Attention! . . . Il s'agit de ne rien casser!

ACTUALITIES.

THE LADY OF THE EGGS.

"Careful! Don't break any of them."   (D. 3537—1866)

L'Equilibre Européen.

ACTUALITIES.

The European Equilibrium. (D. 3540)—1866)

UN BAISER DE CIRCONSTANCE.

ACTUALITIES.

AN EMBRACE OF EXPEDIENCY. (D. 3565—1867)

Ca pousse tout de même fort l'opinion publique.

ACTUALITIES.

Even so, public opinion pushes hard.   (D. 3328—1869)

Comme Sisyphe.

ACTUALITIES.

Like Sisyphus.   (D. 3128—1869)

Je voulais la lui jeter et c'est moi qui me suis sali.

ACTUALITIES.

I wanted to throw it at him, and I muddied myself.   (D. 3308—1869)

UN CAUCHEMAR DE M. DE BISMARCK.

Merci!

ACTUALITIES.

A NIGHTMARE OF BISMARK.

"Thank you!"   (D. 3314—1870)

Comment Bismarck comprend l'unité allemande.

ACTUALITIES.

Bismark's conception of German unity.   (D. 3442—1870)

"Tu resteras dehors et cloué sur la porte."

ACTUALITIES.

"You will stay on the outside, nailed to the door."
March 1, 1871 (Order of the Day of the National Assembly). (D. 3463—1871)

LA MAUDITE!

ACTUALITIES.

THE CURSED YEAR! (D. 3901—1872)

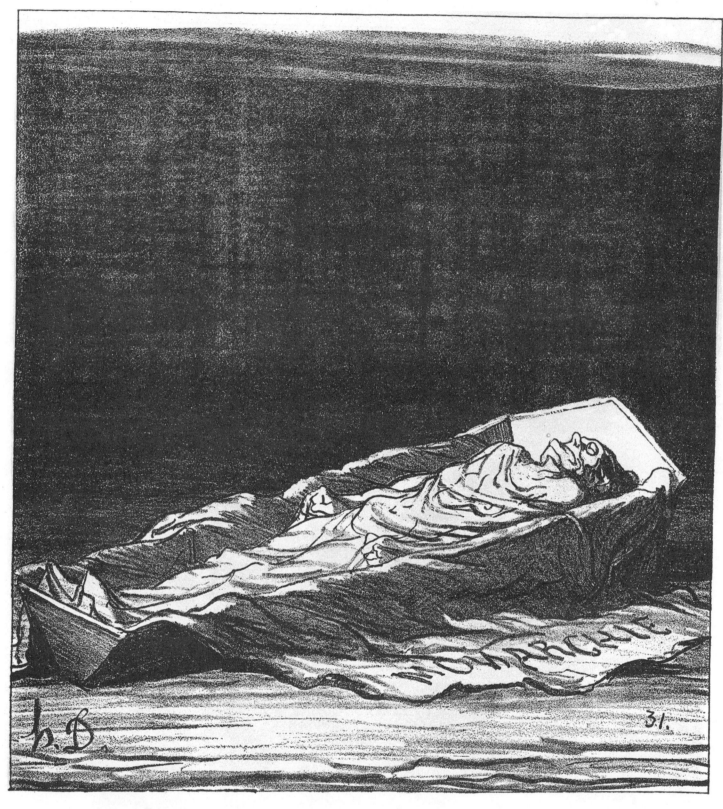

Et pendant ce temps-là, ils continuent à affirmer qu'elle ne s'est jamais mieux portée.

ACTUALITIES.

And during all this time, they kept on saying that he never felt better. (D. 3415—1872)

Daumier's Lawyers and Doctors

Daumier's Lawyers

Daumier had good reason to know intimately the laws and lawyers of Paris. His first job was as an assistant to a notary. His father was always involved in litigation with creditors, and later the artist found himself in the courts for the same reason.

The black-robed functionaries of the law lent themselves very well to lithographic representation, and they appear in numerous plates. The two major series of lithographs concerning lawyers were *Les Gens de Justice* (Men of the Law) and *Les Avocats et les Plaideurs* (Lawyers and Litigants). There were, however, numerous other lithographs and several drawings and paintings concerning lawyers and the courts.

Les Gens de Justice consisted of thirty-eight plates executed from 1845 through 1848. There were five more plates done for the series but never published as part of it. One seldom has to read the caption to gather the meaning of these works. The satisfied smugness of the lawyers and the ignorant corruption of the judges are translated into facial and bodily expressions. The sweeping gestures of the advocates and their mercenary eyes betray their moral emptiness —and Daumier captures it all. The poor are the victims of this vicious system, but even they are not romanticized.

Les Avocats et les Plaideurs was made up of four plates and was published in 1857. The drawings and watercolors that are represented here were done for the most part after 1855. Daumier's attitude had grown more fierce. The officers of the court are no longer amusing. In one watercolor the gowns of the complacent lawyers almost hide a weeping widow.

Daumier's Doctors

There is no major series of lithographs that concerns itself exclusively with doctors, unless one counts the early plates entitled *L'Imagination*. Doctors and the medical fads that swept Parisian society were, however, a fertile field for the times when the government forbade the political caricature.

Daumier is not nearly as savage with the medical men as he is with the men of the legal profession. He employs irony rather than sarcasm in portraying dieting, pregnancy, and hypochondria. The patients from the upper middle class are portrayed less than sympathetically, but the peasant in *Le Malade* is obviously an object of compassion and sympathy.

Though Daumier's personal relations with lawyers were particularly bad, he seems to have been a very healthy man who had little reason to frequent doctors until the end of his life. In the Robert Macaire series which follows this section, the reader will find more plates of medical relevance. These involve a confidence man posing as a doctor, and include a plate which has Macaire remark that his "impossible" operation was a success. When a bystander points out that the patient is dead, Dr. Macaire replies, "So what, she would have died anyhow."

— Perdu, monsieur... perdu sur tous les points..... et vous me disiez encore ce matin que ma cause était excellente!...

— Parbleu... je suis encore tout prêt à le soutenir si vous voulez en appeler.... mais je vous préviens qu'en Cour royale je ne le soutiens pas à moins de cent écus!....

MEN OF JUSTICE.

"Lost on all counts? But you told me again this morning that my case was excellent!"
"To be sure. I am still ready to continue the case if you want to appeal but I warn you, in the Royal Court my fee is at least 330F." (D. 1337—1845)

– Faut-y faire une lettre pour l'attendrir?....
– Attendrir un huissier!.. vous n'êtes donc pas français, mon brave homme?...

MEN OF JUSTICE.

"Can you write a letter to soften him up?"
"Soften up a bailiff! You're not French, my good man?"
(D. 1341—1845)

Un avocat qui évidemment est rempli de la conviction la plus intime............ que son client le paiera bien.

MEN OF JUSTICE.

"He is a lawyer evidently full of such deeply rooted conviction . . . that his client will pay him very well."   (D. 1342—1845)

—*Allons donc, chers confrères . . . vous avez tort de vous disputer hors de l'audience . . . ce lieu ci doit être
la salle des pas perdus pour les plaideurs . . . mais jamais les avocats ne doivent y perdre des paroles . . .*

MEN OF JUSTICE.

"Now then, dear colleagues, you are wrong to dispute without an audience. . . . This is the place where
litigants lose cases . . . but lawyers should never waste their words here." (D. 1343—1845)

Chez Aubert & C⁰ P⁹ de la Bourse 29.

Imp.Mourlot F.ʳˢˢ

— Vous m'avez injurié dans votre plaidoirie, mais je saurai bien vous forcer à m'en rendre raison !...
— Monsieur, apprenez que je ne vous crains pas !.. j'ai au plus haut dégré, le courage civil de ne jamais répondre à une provocation !...

MEN OF JUSTICE.

"You insulted me in your discourse, but I will force you to see the truth."
"I'm not afraid of you! I possess the highest degree of civil courage. I never respond to a challenge."
(D. 1347—1845)

Chez Aubert & Cie Pl. de la Bourse, 29.

Imp. Mourlot Frres

— Oui, on veut dépouiller cet orphelin, que je ne qualifie pas de jeune, puis qu'il a cinquante sept ans, mais il n'en est pas moins orphelin.... je me rassure toute fois, messieurs, car la justice a toujours les yeux ouverts sur toutes les coupables menées !.....

MEN OF JUSTICE.

"Yes, they want to convict this orphan, whom I don't consider young as he is fifty-seven. But he is, nonetheless, still an orphan. I always comfort myself, gentlemen, with the knowledge that judges always look with open eyes upon all the circumstances." (D. 1347—1845)

Chez Aubert & C.ᵉ Pl. de la Bourse, 29.

Imp.Mourlot F.ʳᵉˢ

— Et dire que voilà trois de mes prévenus que je n'ai pas pu faire condamner ! . . . je vais être perdu de réputation ! . . . .

MEN OF JUSTICE.

"And to think that there are three of my defendants whom I could not get condemned! I'm going to lose my reputation!" (D. 1348—1845)

Chez Aubert Pl. de la Bourse, 29 .

Imp. Mourlot F^{res}

– Mon cher que voulez vous . . . . nous avons eu du malheur . . . . je n'ai pas pu prouver votre innocence, cette fois . . . . mais à votre prochain vol j'espère être plus heureux ! . . .

MEN OF JUSTICE.

"My dear friend, what do you expect? We have had a setback. I couldn't prove your innocence this time, but after your next robbery, I hope to be happier!" (D. 1349—1845)

Chez Aubert, Pl. de la Bourse, 29.

Imp.Mourlot, Frès

Dites donc, confrère, vous allez soutenir aujourd'hui contre moi absolument ce que je plaidais il y a trois semaines dans une cause identique.. hé hé hé!.. c'est drôle!..

Et moi je vais vous redebiter ce que vous me ripostiez a cette époque... c'est très amusant, au besoin nous pourrons nous soufler mutuellement.. hi hi hi!..

MEN OF JUSTICE.

"Say, colleague, today you are going to defend against me in the exact same type of case I defended three weeks ago. I say! That's funny."
"I am going to reply with the same words you used then. It's funny. When we have to, we can strike at each other with each other's words." (D. 1350—1845)

Chez Aubert & C. Pl. de la Bourse, 29.

Imp. Mourlot. F.

Vous aviez faim... vous aviez faim... ça n'est pas une raison... mais moi aussi presque tous les jours j'ai faim et je ne vole pas pour cela !.....

MEN OF JUSTICE.

"So you were hungry. That's no excuse. I'm hungry myself almost every day, but I don't steal."
(D. 1351—1845)

Chez Aubert & Cᵗᵉ Pl. de la Bourse 29.

Imp.Mourlot Fʳᵉˢ

M.ʳ l'avocat·a rendu pleine justice au rare talent déployé par le ministère public dans son réquisitoire ; M.ʳ le procureur général s'empresse de rendre un hommage mérité a l'admirable éloquence du défenseur, M.ʳ le président applaudit aux deux orateurs ; bref tout le monde est execssivement satisfait, excepté l'accusé.

MEN OF JUSTICE.

The defense counsel dispensed full justice to the rare talent displayed by the public prosecutor in his indictment. The Attorney General is eager to render merited praise to the admirable eloquence of the counsel for the defense. The presiding judge applauds the two speakers. In conclusion, everyone is extremely satisfied except the accused.   (D. 1352—1846)

Chez Aubert Pl de la Bourse 29.

Imp.Mourlot Frès

– Voyons témom il serait important de nous faire le détail éxact et complet de l'emploi de votre journée du 12 Avril dernier?
– Mais m'sieu le président il y a neuf mois de cela . . . . .
– Ça ne fait rien . . . . . dites toujours ! . . . .

MEN OF JUSTICE.

"Let's see, witness. It would be important for you to give the exact and complete details of your activities on April 12 past."
"But judge, that was nine months ago."
"That doesn't matter. Tell us anyway."   (D. 1353—1846)

Chez Aubert, Pl de la Bourse, 29.

Imp. Mourlot Frères

Maitre Chapotard lisant dans un journal judiciaire l'éloge de lui même par lui même.

MEN OF JUSTICE.

Advocate Chapotard, reading in the lawyer's journal praises of himself . . . written by himself.
(D. 1354—1846)

– Ce qui m'chiffonne c'est que j'suis accusé de douze vols!..
– Il y en a douze… tant mieux…. je plaiderai la monomanie!..

MEN OF JUSTICE.

"What gets me is being accused of twelve robberies."
"There were twelve? Good! I'll plead kleptomania."
(D. 1355—1846)

Mon cher monsieur, il m'est absolument impossible de plaider votre affaire..... il vous manque les pièces les plus importantes...... *(à part)* les pièces de cent sous!.........

MEN OF JUSTICE.

"My dear sir, I cannot possibly take your case. You are missing the most important evidence." (*Aside*) "Evidence of money." (D. 1356—1846)

Chez Aubert & C.ᵉ Pl. de la Bourse. 29.

Imp. d'Aubert & C.ⁱᵉ

—Voilà le ministère public qui vous dit des choses très désagréables......tâchez donc de pleurer au moins d'un œil......ça fait toujours bien!.......

MEN OF JUSTICE.

"There is the public prosecutor who will say disagreeable things about your character. Try to cry a little. That's always good." (D. 1357—1846)

Il défend l'orphelin et la veuve, à moins pourtant qu'il n'attaque la veuve et l'orphelin.

MEN OF JUSTICE.

"He invariably defends the orphans and widows; unless he has been retained to attack them."
(D. 1358—1846)

Chez Aubert & Cie. Pl. de la Bourse.

Imp. d'Aubert & Cie.

— Quel dommage que cette charmante petite femme ne m'ait pas chargé de défendre sa cause....... comme je plaiderais que son mari est un gredin!.....

MEN OF JUSTICE.

"Too bad that charming little woman didn't retain me to defend her. What a pleasure it would have been denouncing her husband."   (D. 1360—1846)

Un plaideur peu satisfait.

MEN OF JUSTICE.

A not very satisfied client. (D. 1362—1846)

Chez Aubert & C.ⁱᵉ Pl. de la Bours. 29.

Imp.Mourlot Fʳᵉˢ

— Plaidez , plaidez..... ça sera un bon tour à jouer à votre voisin ....vous lui ferez manger plus de cent écus!.....
— Oui, mais c'est qu'moi...: j'en mangerais itou des miens.....des écus....et j'ai pas d'appétit pour ça !

MEN OF JUSTICE.

"Sue, Sue. . . . Taking the case to court will be a good trick on your neighbor. We will consume
a lot of his money."
"Yes, but you will eat up mine and I don't relish that."   (D. 1356—1846)

Chez Aubert & Cⁱᵉ Pl de la Bourse 29.

Imp.Mourlot Frᵉˢ

—Laissez dire un peu de mal de vous....laissez dire....tout à l'heure, moi, je vais injurier toute la famille de votre adversaire!...

MEN OF JUSTICE.

"Let him say some bad things about you. Later, *I* am going to insult your adversary's whole family."   (D. 1368—1847)

Une péroraison à la Démosthène.

MEN OF JUSTICE.

A summation in the style of Demosthenes.
(D. 1369—1847)

Chez Aubert Pl. de la Bourse.

Imp. Mourlot Frs.

_ Encore perdu en Cour Royale . . . et il se lamente comme s'il ne lui restait pas encore la Cour de Cassation ! . . .

MEN OF JUSTICE.

"Lost again in the lower courts and he laments as if he couldn't still appeal."
(D. 1370—1848)

Chez Aubert Pl. de la Bourse.   Imp.Mourlot Frères

— Vous avez perdu votre procès c'est vrai......mais vous avez du éprouver bien du plaisir à m'entendre plaider.

MEN OF JUSTICE.

"It's true. You lost your case but you had the pleasure of hearing me plead it."   D. 1371—1848)

Grand escalier du Palais de justice.
Vue de faces.

MEN OF JUSTICE.

The Courthouse Steps.
Survey of faces.   (D. 1372—1848)

Chez Aubert, Pl. de la Bourse.

Imp.Mourlot Frères

— Il paraît décidément que mon gaillard est un grand scélérat . . . . . . tant mieux . . . . si je parviens à le faire acquitter, quel honneur pour moi ! . . . . .

MEN OF JUSTICE.

It seems that my client is a scoundrel. Good.
What honor for me if I get him acquitted!   (D. 1373—1848)

— Vous êtes jolie ..... nous prouverons facilement que votre mari a eu tous les torts !.....

MEN OF JUSTICE.

"You are pretty. We will easily prove that your husband made all the mistakes." (D. 1375—1848)

UNTITLED DRAWING.

L'avocat. — L'affaire marche, l'affaire marche!

Le plaideur. — Vous me dites cela depuis quatre ans; si elle marche encore longtemps comme ça, je finirai par n'avoir plus de bottes pour la suivre!...

LAWYERS AND CLIENTS.

Lawyer—"The case is moving along."
Client—"You have been telling me that for four years. If it continues at this pace, I will no longer have boots to follow it." (D. 2185—1851)

— Ils ont tous des cliens... moi seul n'en ai pas! il faudra que je finisse par commettre quelque forfait pour avoir enfin la satisfaction de me confier ma défense!

LAWYERS AND CLIENTS.

I'm the only one without a client. I'll have to commit some crime to have a case to defend.   (D. 2186—1851)

_Enfin! nous avons obtenu la séparation de biens des deux époux.
_Il est bien temps, le procès les a ruinés tous les deux!

LAWYERS AND CLIENTS.

"Finally! We finished the division of the divorcees' property."
"It's about time, the case ruined both of them." (D. 2187—1851)

_ Ne manquez pas de me répliquer, moi je vous répliquerai...ça nous fera toujours deux plaidoieries de plus à faire payer à nos cliens !..

LAWYERS AND CLIENTS.

"Don't forget to exercise your right of reply. I will exercise mine. That will give our clients two extra speeches to pay for."   (D. 2188—1851)

CONVERSATION BETWEEN LAWYERS.

"MY DEAR FELLOW!"

137

APRES LE PROCES.

AFTER THE HEARING.

APRES LE JUGEMENT.

AFTER THE VERDICT.

LES OBJETS PRODUIT EN EVIDENCE.

THE ARTICLES PRODUCED IN EVIDENCE.

Mr. PRUNE.

MR. PRUNE. (D. 60—1833)

Mme de la Piçonnerie, accoucheuse jurée, prend des pensionnaires à juste prix.

MIDWIFE.

Madame de la Piçonnerie takes in lodgers for a fair price.
(D. 155—1833)

Imp. Mourlot Frès

LE MALADE

THE SICK MAN. (D. 255—1835)

Imp. Mourlot F^{res}

La Potion | *Draught.*

MEDICINE. (D. 327—1836)

Une envie de femme grosse.

MARRIED LIFE.

CRAVINGS OF A PREGNANT WOMAN. (D. 638—1839)

Imp. Mourlot F^{res}

Elle tenait ferme!...

GROTESQUE SCENES.

"It certainly was solid."   (D. 732—1839)

Le Malade imaginaire.

Imp. Mourlot Frères

THE HYPOCHONDRIAC. (D. 864—1841)

LE STRABISME,

– Ma foi je ne vous reconnaissais pas ! – Ah ! c'est que je me suis fait opérer, je ne louche plus, ça me change tout-
à-fait n'est-ce-pas ! – Oh ! tout-à-fait, car avant vous louchiez en dehors je crois .....

ACTUALITIES.

THE SQUINT.

"Lord, I didn't recognize you."
"Oh, that's because I had an operation. I'm no longer cross-eyed, and that changes my looks completely,
don't you think?"
"Yes, completely. Before, you squinted toward the outside." (D. 916—1841)

Imp. Mourlot Fʳᵉˢ

UNE HEUREUSE TROUVAILLE.

Parbleu je suis ravi..... vous avez la fièvre jaune.....c'est la première fois de ma vie que j'ai le bonheur d'en soigner une !

RED LETTER DAYS.

A LUCKY FIND.

"By Jove, I'm delighted. You have yellow fever—it will be my first opportunity to treat this disease!"
(D. 1110—1844)

LES CIGARETTES DE CAMPHRE.

— On m'a certifié que c'etait excellent pour engraisser !..
— On m'a juré que c'etait souverain pour faire maigrir !..

RED LETTER DAYS.

CAMPHOR CIGARETTES.

"I've been told they're wonderful for putting on weight."
"And I've been assured that they're infallible for reducing."   (D. 1169—1846)

PARIS GRIPPÉ.

_ Comment toussez -vous ?......
_ Vous êtes bien bonne...,je tousse assez bien...... et vous ?....

PARISIAN SKETCHES.

PARIS GRIPPE.

"How are you coughing?"
"You are very kind. I'm coughing very well . . . and you?" (D. 3022—1858)

Imp. Mourlot Frès

La Colique

Hola! hola!..... hola! le ventre!.... hola!!

THE IMAGINATION.

CRAMPS.

"Oh!—my stomach!"   (D. 34—1833)

Le mal de tête.

Hola! hola! . . . pan! pan! . . . dindrelindin — dindrelindin. hola! hola! hola!!

Imp. Mourlot Frès

THE IMAGINATION.

THE HEADACHE.

"Oh! bang! bang! . . . ding! dong! Oh!" (D. 37—1833)

Le malade imaginaire.

Imp. Mourlot Fres

THE IMAGINATION.

THE HYPOCHONDRIAC.

I'm finished. I'll make my will. They will bury me. Farewell.   (D. 38—1833)

Le médecin,

Pourquoi, diable! mes malades s'en vont ils donc tous?.............. j'ai beau les saigner, les purger, les droguer.......... je n'y comprends rien!

Imp. Mourlot Frès

THE IMAGINATION.

THE DOCTOR.

How can it be that all my patients die? I bleed them,
I physic them, I drug them. I simply don't understand. (D. 43—1833)

ROBERT MACAIRE, PHILANTHROPIST.

"You see, Bertrand, we are moralists in the market. We will treat the stockholders free of charge;
you will purge them, I will bleed them." (D. 355—1836)

Robert Macaire

In 1823, the great actor Frédérick Lemaître portrayed the role of a desperate escaped convict completely without scruples who finally turns on his criminal confederates. The play was titled *L'auberge des Adrets,* but the only memorable part of it was Lemaître's performance as Robert Macaire.

Lemaître had at one time seen a vagrant who wore nothing ". . . but rags and tatters, but how magnificently he carried them off." He was eating a pastry, ". . . holding it daintily in fingers the tips of which stuck out of their gloves." This tramp with style became the basis of the actor's characterization. Macaire became such a popular rage that Lemaître himself collaborated on another play entitled *Robert Macaire.* This version was produced in 1834 and was also highly successful.

Daumier and Philipon, his publisher, had been casting about for some means of attacking the government and the greedy, unscrupulous bureaucracy that supported it. Philipon began writing captions for a series of lithographs to be based on the Lemaître character, and Daumier produced the first drawings in 1836. Macaire was no longer a violent criminal; instead, he had become an instrument to part fools from their money. Daumier produced one hundred drawings for the Macaire series between 1836 and 1838. Later he was to add twenty more.

The lithographs, like the play that inspired them, were instant hits. People clamored for the latest Macaire exploit, and the swindler was seen in guises ranging from dentist to matchmaker. His crony Bertrand is often present to serve as his master's foil, almost a Gallic Sancho Panza, as Mr. and Mrs. Getlein point out in their appreciation.

Daumier did not like sticking to the Macaire format. Philipon, on the other hand, was only too eager to take credit for the inspiration and genius in the series. At times he insisted that the captions rather than the drawings made Macaire such a popular character.

Macaire satirizes not only the amoral con man but also, as in Twain's works, his victim who desires something for nothing. Speculation was rampant in France during those years, and many Frenchmen must have recognized themselves in the series. Mr. Getlein points out how the "Macaire line" survived the particular character and was carried over to the figures in the drawings of some of Daumier's lawyers and tradesmen.

Robert Macaire M^d de Bibles.

Chez Aubert gal Vero dodat. *par Mrs Daumier et Philippon.*

(*Bertrand*) Les souscripteurs disent que nous sommes des farceurs, que nous nous f..... fichons deux et ils nous f..... fichent à la porte..... (*Robert Macaire*) De quelles expressions vous servez vous diable!.... parlez plus décemment devant moi ou je vous f... fi.... flanque par la fenêtre........ ce sont vos airs mondains, vos paroles mondaines qui scandalisent les souscripteurs, retournez y..... s'ils vous fichent à la porte, rentrez par la fenêtre s'ils vous fichent un soufflet, tendez l'autre joue..... mais, ne revenez pas sans abonnements, malheureux ou je vous f..... ma malédiction!

ROBERT MACAIRE, BIBLE SALESMAN.

(*Bertrand*) "The subscribers say we are swindlers, that we cheat them."
(*Robert Macaire*) "What kind of language is this? It's only your modern ways and your soft songs which make the subscribers so angry. Stop it. If they throw you out the door come back in the window, but whosoever shall smite you on your cheek, turn to him the other cheek also . . . but don't come back without new subscribers, you wretch, or you'll be hanged."
(D. 444—1838)

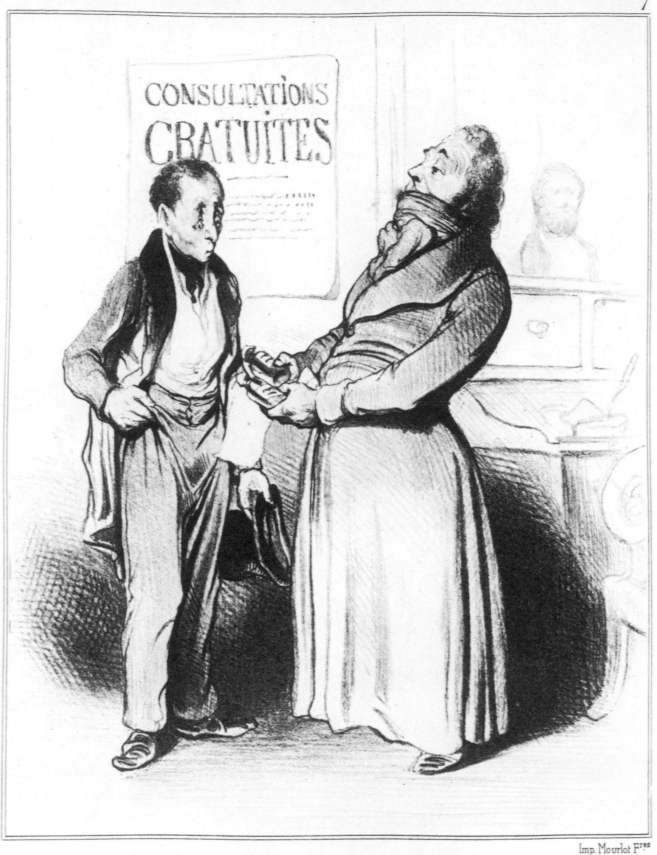

Imp. Mourlot F^res

Diable! ne plaisantez pas avec cette maladie!..... Croyez moi, buvez de l'eau, beaucoup d'eau. Frottez vous les os des jambes et revenez me voir souvent, ça ne vous ruinera pas mes consultations sont gratuites..... .....Vous me devez 20.^f pour ces deux bouteilles. (On reprend le verre pour 10 centimes)

"Don't take this sickness lightly! Believe me, drink water, lots of water! Rub the bones of your legs, and come to see me often. That won't make you poor, my consultations are free. Now, you owe me 20 francs for these two bottles (this includes 10 centimes deposit on the containers)." (D. 361—1936)

Imp. Mourlot F^{res}

Un Oculiste breveté.

Ah! ça, Monsieur Macaire, depuis six mois vous me bassinez avec votre eau merveilleuse et je suis toujours aveugle. Cela finit par me couter bien cher, mon argent s'en va, c'est tout ce que je vois — . . . Eh bien! c'est déjà quelque chose; continuez, vous finirez par y voir clair . . . (à Part) dans votre bourse.

A LICENSED OPTOMETRIST.

"Listen, Mr. Macaire, for six months now you've been promising me wonders from your eyewash and I'm still blind. It's costing me a lot and all I see is my money melting away."

"Well, that's something, keep on and you'll get to where you'll see clearly . . . (*aside*) to the bottom of your pocketbook."

(D. 410—1837)

Robert Macaire Dentiste.

Saprebleu ! M. le dentiste, vous m'avez arraché deux bonnes dents et vous avez laissé les deux mauvaises... (Rob. M. à part) Diable !! (haut) sans doute ! et j'avais mes raisons... nous sommes toujours à temps d'arracher les mauvaises... quand aux autres, elles auraient fini par se gâter et par vous faire mal... Un ratelier postiche ne vous fera jamais souffrir et c'est bien meilleur genre, on ne porte plus que ça.

ROBERT MACAIRE, DENTIST.

"Good God, Doctor! You pulled out two good teeth and left the two bad ones."
(*Rob. M. aside*) "I'll be damned! (*aloud*) Of course I did, for good reason. There'll be plenty of time to pull out the bad ones . . . the others would have decayed and caused you pain eventually. A dental plate never hurts and it's right in style."
(D. 412—1837)

Clinique du Docteur Robert-Macaire.

Hé bien! Messieurs, vous l'avez vú, cette opération qu'on disait impossible a parfaitement réussi....—
Mais, monsieur, la malade est morte......—Qu'importe! Elle serait bien plus morte sans l'opération

Imp. Mourlot Frès

DR. ROBERT MACAIRE'S CLINIC.

"There you are, gentlemen. You've seen this operation, that everyone said was impossible, performed with complete success."
"But, doctor, the patient is dead."
"So what! She would have died anyway, even without the operation."   (D. 418—1837)

Imp. Mourlot F^{res}

Le public, mon cher, le public est stupide.... nous le saignons à blanc, nous le purgeons à mort, il n'est pas content.... il veut du nouveau... donnons lui en, morbleu, du nouveau! faisons nous homéopates.— Similia Similibus.—(Bertrand) Amen!.— Tiens, voici une ordonnance qui résume le système: Prendre un zour petit grain de.... de rien du tout.... le couper en dix millions de molécules.... jeter une.... une seule! de ces dix millionnièmes parties dans la rivière.... remuer, remuer, triturer beaucoup.... laisser infuser quelques heures.... puiser un seau de cette eau bienfaisante.... la filtrer.... la couper avec 20 parties d'eau ordinaire et s'en humecter la langue tous les matins, à jeun.... Voila!.— Est ce tout? — Oui... Ah! diable! j'oubliai le principal.... Payer la présente ordonnance.

"The public, old chap, is stupid. We bleed it, physic it to death, and it's not satisfied. It wants a change. Let's give it something new and become homeopaths . . . *Similia Similibus.*
(*Bertrand*) "Amen!"
"Here's a prescription that sums it up—Take a tiny grain of nothing at all—separate it into 10 million molecules—throw one —just one—of these ten-millionth parts into the river—stir until well mixed—let steep several hours—fill a pail with healing water—filter—dilute with 20 parts ordinary water—and wet the tongue with it before breakfast."
"Is that all?"
"Yes. Oh, I forgot the most important part—pay for the prescription." (D. 425—1837)

Imp. Mourlot Fres

Recette pour guérir la colique.

Mr Macaire, mon cher ami, ne me faites pas manquer cette soirée, j'en ai tant besoin. — Ah mon ami, je ne puis jouer, je souffre trop.... — Essayez, je vous en conjure.... le public vous demande, il crie, menace, veut briser les banquettes, je vais être forcé de rendre l'argent.... voyons je doublerai vos feux.... — Oh là ! Oh là !.... chauffez des serviettes !.... du vin chaud !.... chauffez, chauffez !!! — Je triplerai vos feux.... — Chauffez toujours, chauffez ! ..... chauffez les serviettes.... — Nous partagerons la recette........ — Nous partagerons la recette ? levez le rideau, la farce est jouée, le drame commence........

HOW TO CURE CRAMPS.

"Mr. Macaire, my good friend, don't miss this performance, I need it badly."

"I can't go on, I'm in too much pain."

"Try, I beg you, the public wants you. They're shouting and ready to rip the seats. I'll have to return their money. I'll double your bonus."

"Oh, heat some towels, bring hot wine."

"I'll triple your bonus."

"Keep the heat on. Keep heating the towels."

"We'll share the receipts."

"We'll share the receipts? Up with the curtain, the farce is ended, the drama begins."   (D. 427—1837)

Robert Macaire magnétiseur.

Imp. Mourlot F^res

Voici un excellent sujet ... pour le magnétisme ... Certes, il n'y pas de commérage, je n'ai pas l'honneur de connaître Mlle de St Bertrand et vous allez voir Messieurs, l'effet du somnambulisme.
(Mlle de St Bertrand donne dans son sommeil des consultations sur les maladies de chacun, indique des trésors cachés sous terre et conseille de prendre des actions dans le papier Mozart, dans les mines d'or et dans une foule d'autres fort belles opérations.)

ROBERT MACAIRE, HYPNOTIST.

"Here is an excellent subject for hypnotism. There's no connivance; I don't even know Mlle. de St. Bertrand; you will see the effects of trance. (Mlle. de St. Bertrand in her sleep gives consultation on illness, tells where treasures are hidden, advises buying stock in the Mozart Paper Co., gold mines, and some other fine enterprises.")   (D. 443—1838)

Le Début.

(Bertrand) Oh! non la malade est faible, elle succomberait..... l'opération devient impraticable...
(Robt Mac.) Impraticable!!!.. il n'y a rien d'impraticable pour un débutant... Ecoute! nous sommes inconnus, si nous échouons, nous restons dans l'obscurité; ça ne nous recule pas si par hasard, nous réussissons...... C'est fini, nous sommes lancés, notre réputation est faite!.. (Ensemble) Pratiquons! pratiquons.

(Donnez donc votre pratique à ces gaillards là.

Imp. Mourlot F^{res}

THE BEGINNER.

(*Bertrand*) "No, the patient is too weak, she wouldn't survive; the operation is impracticable."
(*Robt. Mac.*) "Nothing is impracticable for a beginner. We have no standing yet in the profession. If we fail, we lose nothing. If, by chance, we succeed . . . we'll be on our way, our reputation will be made."
(*Both*) "Let's go ahead, then."   (D. 430—1838)

ROBERT MACAIRE ARCHITECTE.

ROBERT MACAIRE, ARCHITECT.

Comment, Mr. Macaire, cette maison qui ne devait me coûter, d'après votre devis, que 70,000 fr. va me revenir à plus de trois cent mille? . . . —Que voulez vous, ce n'est pas ma faute, vous faites percer au midi une croisée que nous devions ouvrir au nord; vous ne voulez plus que quatre étages au lieu de cinq; nous devions couvrir en zinc, nous ne couvrons plus qu'en ardoise. Je ne puis répondre que mon projet, vous le changez, ça vous regarde.

"But, Mr. Macaire, this house should have cost me only 70,000 francs according to your estimate. Now it will set me back more than 300,000."

"It's not my fault. You wanted a window placed to catch the noon sun, but our standard windows open only to the north; you wanted only four stories, instead of five; we had to cover the roof in zinc for you and our standard covering is slate. All I can say, sir, is that you made the changes, it's your responsibility." (D. 395—1837)

167

"And so what . . . so what . . . your dowry! Has it perhaps been eaten, your dowry? It has been lost in industrial transactions and besides—does a dowry last forever? I am thinking of making use of several." (D. 390—1837)

Monsieur Daumier, votre série des Robert Macaire est une chose charmante! . . . C'est la peinture exacte des voleries de notre époque. . . . C'est le portrait fidèle d'une foule de coquins qu'on retrouve partout, dans le commerce, dans la politique, dans le barreau, dans la finance, partout! partout!!! . . . Les fripons doivent bien vous en vouloir. . . . Mais l'estime des honnêtes gens vous est acquise. . . . Vous n'avez pas encore la croix d'honneur? . . . C'est révoltant!!!

"M. Daumier, your series of Robert Macaire is perfectly charming. You have captured the viciousness of our era. It's a faithful portrait of the crowd of scoundrels that one finds everywhere; in business, in politics, in the law, banking, everywhere, everywhere!! Those rascals must wish you ill, but you have the esteem of honest men everywhere. Have you not yet been given the Croix d'Honneur? Isn't that sickening?" (D. 433—1838)

ROBERT MACAIRE.

ROBERT MACAIRE.

Salut! terre de l'hospitalité . . . salut! patrie de ceux qui n'en ont plus . . . asile sacré des malheureux que la justice humaine proscrit . . . salut!!! A tous les coeurs fanés que la Belgique est chère.

"Greetings, land of hospitality! Greetings, land of those who have nothing left . . . sacred refuge of those whom human justice has abandoned . . . Greetings! To all withered hearts, Belgium is precious." (D. 866—1840)

Robert Macaire Notaire.

Ce sublime Macaire, toi Notaire de toute la banque, des banquistes, créateur des bénéfices chippés, des frimes de toute couleur et de toute grandeur, tu es calomnié tu passes pour un Palloquet!...... Ingratitude de la Société .... en commandite!!

ROBERT MACAIRE, NOTARY PUBLIC.

"Oh, splendid Macaire, solicitor of the stock exchange and swindlers. You who invented new types of bribes and phony balance sheets. Now you are slandered. Oh, the ingratitude of business-men."   (D. 358—1836)

Robert-Macaire agent matrimonial.

ROBERT MACAIRE, MATCHMAKER.

"Mr. Gobard, I have the honor to present you to Mme. de St. Bertrand, widow of the Grand Army. She is very wealthy. Also I would like to present Mlle. Wormspire, daughter of the famous Baron of Wormspire. She has been granted an annuity of 50,000 livres. These ladies are very anxious to meet you. I have asked them to dine at your house and then you will take us to the opera after which we will play some cards. Mr. Gobard, these ladies have plans for you; show yourself at your best." (D. 369—1836)

Robert-Macaire Avocat.

Mon cher Bertrand, donnes moi cent écus, je te fais acquitter d'emblée. — J'ai pas d'argent. Eh bien donne moi cent francs. — pas le sou. — tu n'as pas dix francs? pas un liard! alors donne moi les bottes je te plaiderai la circonstance atténuante.

ROBERT MACAIRE, LAWYER.

"My dear Bertrand, give me a hundred ecus and I will have you acquitted on the spot."

"I have no money."

"All right, give me a hundred francs."

"I don't have a cent."

"You don't have ten francs?"

"Not a penny."

"Well, give me your shoes and I'll plead extenuating circumstances."   (D. 362—1836)

TRIUMPH OF HONESTY IN POLITICS, COMMERCE, LITERATURE, Etc. . . .

(*Very loud*) "My friends, my good friends, you reward me too generously for my work. Very nobly you take revenge on my enemies. My friends, I am all embarrassed and bewildered. (*Low*) Quick, quick, Bertrand, push the wheel, push hard!" (D. 449—1838)

Sculpture, Paintings, Watercolors and Drawings

By Bruce and Seena Harris

As the following plates indicate, Honoré Daumier was one of the most versatile artists of his era. He was not satisfied to accept the commercial rewards of cartooning and lithography, and so turned to other media to find fulfillment. The public, however, was uninterested in his experiments with sculpture, drawing or painting, and yet Daumier did not want his artistic reputation to rest on his lithographs. He hated the economic necessity that forced him to turn out thousands of plates when his instincts and talents drove him to paint. The popular taste of his time devoured the lithographs and scorned his attempts with oil. Daumier persisted, however, and left a body of work that stands above that of his contemporaries and points the way to Impressionism and beyond. His versatility extended into almost every field of the plastic arts. We have included examples from each of his other mediums because they are so beautiful in themselves, and give perspective to his more famous lithographic work.

Sculpture

In Daumier's time there was a Parisian vogue for small terra-cotta figurines which would be placed in shop windows to draw crowds. Philipon persuaded Daumier to do a series of figurines based on leaders of the right. These marvelous sculptures are very close to the lithographic work Daumier was turning out at the time. They constitute not only a political comment but three-dimensional portraits of repulsive qualities. Physiology, in almost an occult sense, fascinated Daumier, and, in his sculpture more than in his other works, one can see emotions and mental states take on physical being. Daumier made forty-five of these small statues and numerous other figures. Bronze casts have been made of the terra-cotta originals in order to preserve these little masterpieces.

Paintings

Daumier tried throughout his lifetime to make his living as a painter. But the public was indifferent to his oils, and it wasn't until 1878 that his friends were able to organize his first show. By that time Daumier had lost his sight and was unable to attend or to read the rather good reviews the show received. The paintings were exhibited with Daumier's rough sketches and the critics spent more time praising the preparatory works. By 1888 the climate of opinion had warmed somewhat, and the critic Arsène Alexandre wrote, "It is this original side of his work (i.e., painting) which finally makes him the equal of the most famous and will open the portals of all the Museums for him when the impartial judgment of posterity has rid the nineteenth century of many other exaggerated reputations. . . ." Daumier's reputation as a painter is now secure, and his works are in the best of the world's museums. Much of his work seems to have been ahead of its time, and in subject matter, feeling, and versatility, his like was not to be seen again until Spain gave us another painter of clowns and Quixotes—Pablo Picasso.

Watercolors and Drawings

Since the original drawings for Daumier's lithographs were done directly on stone, there are no artist's proofs or other "originals." The only impressions we have are the actual newspaper copies. Daumier often made drawings and used these as a basis for his oils. His watercolors were fairly popular, and during the period that *Le Charivari* was not accepting his lithographs these were the artist's main source of income. The drawings and watercolors have a less dramatic and more open feeling than the lithographs. Daumier did not have to resort to caricature in its worst sense and could forgo comic and sensational aspects in deference to purely aesthetic criteria.

Ratapoil
The Walters Art Gallery
Baltimore, Maryland

Ratapoil
The National Gallery of Art,
Washington, D.C.,
Rosenwald Collection

Le Petit Propriétaire
The National Gallery of Art,
Washington, D.C.,
Rosenwald Collection

Le Dandy
The National Gallery of Art,
Washington, D.C.,
Rosenwald Collection

Le Dédaigneux
Collection Joseph H. Hirshorn,
New York

Le Mauvais
Collection Joseph H. Hirshorn,
New York

Le Rieur Edenté
*Collection Joseph H. Hirshorn,
New York*

Le Hargneux
*Collection Joseph H. Hirshorn,
New York*

L'Esprit Fin et Tranchant
Collection Joseph H. Hirshorn,
New York

Crispin and Scapin

Theatre Scene

The Third Class Carriage

The Strong Man of the Fair

The Print Collector
(Oil)

The Connoisseurs
(Oil)

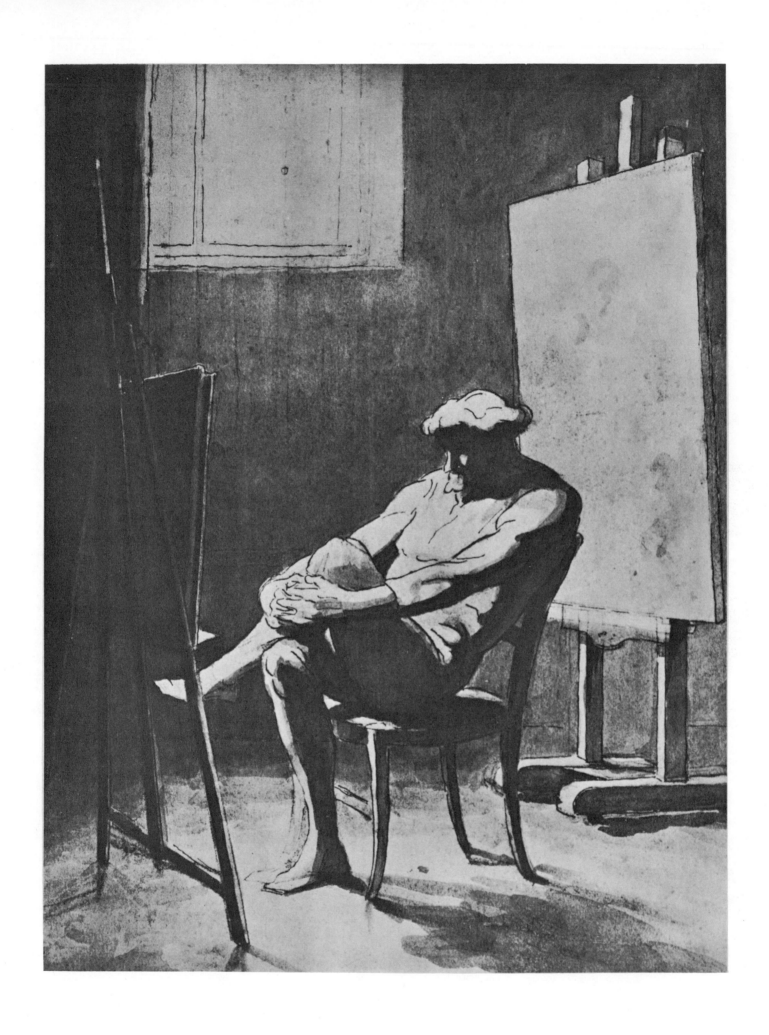

The Artist Before His Work
(Watercolor)

The Painter
(Oil on Wood)

Politics
(Watercolor)

Before the Print-Seller's
(Oil)

In a Painter's Studio
(Watercolor)

Study of a Head
(India Ink)

The Collector
(Watercolor)

The Listener
(Charcoal)

Study of Two Heads
(Drawing)

Archimedes
(Charcoal)

The Third-Class Carriage
(Watercolor)

Circus Parade
(India Ink)

Centaur Ravishing a Nymph
(Drawing)

Riders
(Drawing)

The Kiss
(Charcoal)

The Burden
(Oil)

The Burden
(Terra Cotta)
The Walters Art Gallery, Baltimore, Maryland

199

Parade of the Mountebanks
(Oil)

Mountebanks Moving
(Drawing with Watercolor)

The Street Singers
(Watercolor)

A Free Show
(Oil)

The Show
(Drawing)

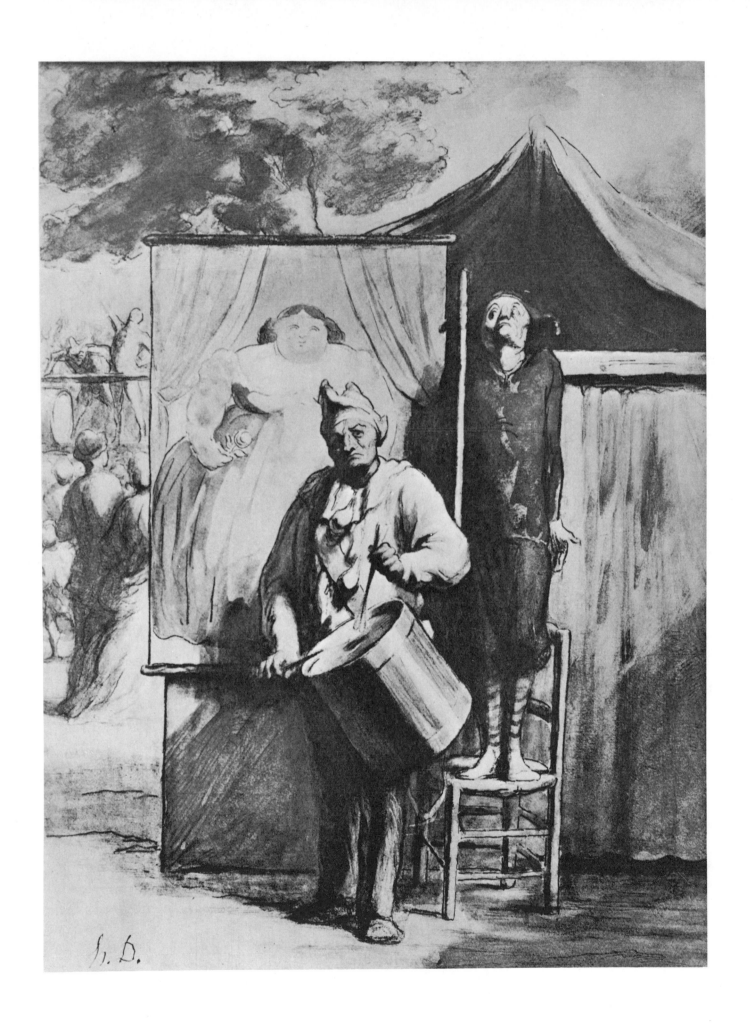

The Show
(Watercolor)

Don Quixote in the Mountains
(Oil on Wood)

Don Quixote and Sancho Panza
(Oil on Wood)

Notes and Historical Explanations

1.
First lithograph which can be conclusively attributed to Daumier.

5.
The long nose of the Count d'Argout was one of Daumier's joys.

6.
The historian Guizot was Minister of Public Instruction.

10.
Baron Joseph de Podernas.

11.
The figure on the left is Louis-Philippe. He is being egged on by Persil to attack the press, but another minister, Guizot, is holding him back.

12.
The Marquis de La Fayette died on May 20, 1834. Before his death, he had come into sharp conflict with Louis-Philippe shortly after the July Revolution, and he had become chief of the opposition.

13.
This pictures the bloody episode that ended a series of attempts at insurrection.

15.
The Spanish king Ferdinand VII left the finances of Spain in terrible disarray. The Count of Toreno, President of the Council, proposed that Spain repudiate all foreign debts incurred by Ferdinand and honor only those incurred by the Cortès, the Spanish parliament.

16.
Refers to the yearly attempts of republicans to resist Louis-Philippe.

18.
The men in political opposition, arrested as a result of troubles of April, 1834, were tried before the French chamber equivalent to the House of Lords. At that time, the Marquis de Barbé-Marbois was ninety years old.

19.
Louis-Philippe teetering between freedom and repression.

20.
In 1832, Daumier was sentenced to six months' imprisonment because of a caricature of Louis-Philippe. He served this in the debtor's jail of Sainte-Pélagie. The figure on the right represents the artist.

31.
Daumier frequently jeered at Victor Hugo, and often with much justice. But he hardly had any right to condemn Hugo's enthusiasm for "fresh flesh," because Daumier himself was inspired by scenes of butchery.

33.
A satire on Hugo's efforts to revive the classic theatre.

73.
The magazine *Le Constitutionnel* aligned itself more and more closely to the fortunes of the prince-president, because its director, Dr. Veron, wished, as he put it, "to be on the winning side."

74.
Daumier had bestowed the characteristics of splendid potbelly, helmet, and gag on the *Constitutionnel* well before the entrance of Dr. Veron onto the scene. The corpulence of the doctor and his fidelity to the same type of shirt collar—characteristics so dear to the caricaturist—permitted Daumier to kill two birds with one stone, and to evoke both the *Constitutionnel* and its new proprietor with the same set of characteristics.

76.
The new legislation against the press exposed newspapers to suppression by simple administrative decision.

77.
This is an allusion to the efforts of the Orleanist Guizot and the legitimist Berryer to unite the two

branches of the Bourbon family, with a view toward restoring the monarchy.

78.

The Bonapartist agents circulated at that time a petition calling for the restoration of the presidential powers of Louis-Napoleon. The creation of the character "Ratapoil" (hairy rat) awoke the enthusiasm of Michelet. He said to Daumier: "You have captured the enemy. The Bonapartist idea will stand forever pilloried by you."

79.

The prognostication of Dr. Veron wasn't quite so bad as that; the Republic still had four months left.

81.

After the coup d'etat, Daumier again had to renounce political caricature.

82.

For two or three years, the crinoline skirt served as a major inspiration for caricaturists.

84.

Ferdinand II, King of the Two Sicilys (King Bomba), took for his motto: "Neither revolution, nor the foreigner." In this plate, Daumier flicks his rapier on Ferdinand's propensity for acting with a heavy hand.

86.

An entryway with turnstile had just been set up at the Stock Exchange. It provided Daumier with an occasion for satirizing the new-fangled turnstile.

87.

The physician Jacques Babinot, of the Academy of Sciences, who was a bit of a charlatan, had intrigued the public with his prediction that the Charles-Quint Comet would appear on June 13, 1857.

91.

With the help of a newly invented rifle, the Prussian Army had conquered Austria shortly before this drawing appeared.

92.

The Peace of Prague has just been declared, and the Franco-Prussian conflict is about to begin. The figure of Diplomacy, in the person of an aged and haggard coquette, was always dear to Daumier.

94.

A general truce was called on the occasion of the Exposition of 1867.

95.

The Government dreaded the approaching general elections. And with some reason; in the elections of May, 1869, the opposition had substantial success.

100.

This plate was published in the *Charivari,* March 1, 1871, at the very moment of the entrance of the German Army into Paris. That same day, the National Assembly, during the course of peace negotiations, confirmed the dethronement of the Emperor, who was declared "responsible for the ruin, the invasion, and the dismemberment of France."

102.

This, the last plate published by Daumier. It appeared in the *Charivari,* September 24, 1872.

142.

Field Marshal Bugeaud had been placed in charge of guarding the Duchesse de Berry under the pretext of supervising her confinement.